DIVORCE OR MARRIAGE

HOWARD L. BASS, currently practicing law in New York City, has lectured and published articles on marriage and divorce. He helped organize the first New York State Conference on Marriage and Divorce, sponsored by N.O.W., leading to divorce reform, and has given recitals of and published poems about the family.

M. L. REIN is a practicing attorney in New York City and was formerly Clerk of the Matrimonial Part of the Supreme Court, State of New York. He is a Fellow of the American Academy of Matrimonial Lawyers.

DIVORCE
OR MARRIAGE
A Legal Guide

HOWARD L. BASS

M. L. REIN

A SPECTRUM BOOK

PRENTICE-HALL, INC., ENGLEWOOD CLIFFS, N.J.

Library of Congress Cataloging in Publication Data

Bass, Howard L
    Divorce or marriage.

    (A Spectrum Book)
    Includes index.
       1. Divorce—United States.   2. Separation (Law)—
United States.   3. Husband and wife—United States.
I. Rein, M. L., joint author.   II. Title.
KF535.B37   346'.73'016   76-14393
ISBN 0-13-216390-0

Prentice-Hall International, Inc., *London*
Prentice-Hall of Australia Pty. Limited, *Sydney*
Prentice-Hall of Canada, Ltd., *Toronto*
Prentice-Hall of India Private Limited, *New Delhi*
Prentice-Hall of Japan, Inc., *Tokyo*
Prentice-Hall of Southeast Asia Pte. Ltd., *Singapore*

Neither the authors nor the publisher intend to offer the information contained in this book as legal advice, which can be offered only by an attorney licensed to practice in your state. Although it is the right of every citizen to inform himself of the law, he can use that information in a court of law only on his own behalf. In addition, there is no guarantee, expressed or implied, that the information contained in this book will be applicable in all details after publication because of the change in the law and in interpretations of the law by the courts. Any inadvertent errors that may have occurred in spite of careful scrutiny are regretted by the authors but cannot cause liability on their part for loss or damages resulting from the use of this material.

Contents

Preface

The purpose of this book is to furnish the layman with a practical guide to the legal intricacies of the marriage-divorce-financial-custody problems that have exploded in family disunity in the last decade.

Every effort has been made to define legal terms in everyday language. The concepts used are simplified so that no legal training is necessary to understand them.

When people are confronted with problems concerning marriage, they may refer to the appropriate section of this book to learn, with reasonable accuracy, what the courts will do if legal action is brought. The book may also guide the reader in finding an amicable approach to resolving both emotional and legal problems that could possibly be avoided. It is hoped that this book will make legal action unnecessary in many situations. At any rate, it is our hope that, when marital difficulties arise, people will turn to this book before taking drastic action on their own, and perhaps even before consulting a lawyer.

However, the book is no substitute for the individual legal advice that a qualified attorney can provide, taking into account the unique personalities of the parties concerned and the singularity of their legal problems.

I. Marriage: Yesterday, Today, and Tomorrow

The word "marriage" has a dual meaning, one denoting the act of entering into the relationship of marriage, and the other, the relationship itself. In a legal marriage a man and woman are united for life under an obligation to discharge to one another and to the community duties which the particular community, by its laws, imposes.

Aside from its religious nature, if any, marriage is a civil contract that requires the consent of the parties involved. But marriage is more than a personal commitment between two people or an economic device contrived by local government to regulate the property rights of its citizens. Marriage has been, and seemingly will continue to be, the basis of the family and, in turn, the foundation of an organized society. The state has always regulated and defined the status of marriage based upon principles of public policy, in an effort to protect the welfare of the citizens. It has the power to determine the conditions on which a marriage may be contracted. Thus the state becomes a silent partner in every wedding of a woman and man.

As part of this book we will discuss the many legal concepts and laws pertaining to the marital relationship, with a general review of each spouse's rights.

Divorce is not a new phenomenon. But in the past few decades marriage seems to have become more and more difficult to maintain than ever before. Why? The major share of difficulties in marriage are results of our own developmental problems. Are we sufficiently aware of ourselves to assume the responsibilities of a marriage? If so, can marriage offer what we need for the fullest completion of our life?

Recent statistical surveys in the United States show that over 35 percent of marriages end in divorce within the first decade of their existence. In 1975 there were more divorces than new marriages, and in recent surveys of state bar associations involved in family law, it has been projected that in the next few years the divorce rate will be 50 percent. In addition, no one would deny the sad truth that many of the marriages that still hold together are far from living up to the original, and often unrealistic, expectations of the partners.

Yet marriage continues to be popular. In our society it is a self-motivated and free-chosen method of trying to achieve human fulfillment and security in the midst of twentieth-century alienation. Most first marriages occur between the ages of 18 and 25. Statistical facts as well as good common sense tell us that the choice of partner, made at this point in our maturation process, is motivated to a great extent by unconscious forces that dwell below our conscious level of awareness. Choices made at this time usually are not based on the realities of a relationship experienced later on.

What are these unconscious forces that drive us to marry? Besides the natural tendency to imitate what we saw in our family as children, there is the need to procreate. In times past, marriages were arranged by third parties. Young women and men did not choose each other—they were "matched" by others who were motivated by a basic need to insure a continuance of healthy bloodlines and long-term family prosperity. Today these needs, though still somewhat active, have been modified. For one thing, there are the realities of an over-populated world. For another, the contemporary idea of romantic love dictates that people themselves should be able to choose the "life partner." The momentary feeling of oneness experienced by those who "fall" in love is very real. But how many are prepared, in this time of the instant love syndrome, to deal with the fact that that first romantic passion soon fades with the some-times harsh reality of living together in day-to-day life? So often we hear people complain about the disappoint-ments of love. But did they consider what this love was all about when it first arrived? Most likely not. The key to the disenchantment lies in the initial lack of aware-ness when the choice was made. Yet, how then could one feel so strongly?

The answer lies within each of us. We all have a cumulative image of the opposite sex imprinted within our being. When we meet our purported match, we tend to unknowingly project a great deal of that inner image. In fact, the very attraction must necessarily have been triggered by some part of this imprint. Thus a girl's image of her husband is likely to be partly predetermined by her prior relationship with her father. A boy's image of his wife is based to a degree upon his developmental relationship with his mother. Whether or not healthy and constructive interactions existed between individuals and those responsible for their nurturing, the fact is that everyone enters into marriage with a predetermined set of images, ideas, and expectations for their marital partner.

Today the tremendous increase in the divorce rate reflects the search for self of men and women. All too often, the romance in a new young marriage, and the stresses involved in rearing children and earning a living, prevent people from paying attention to their needs to be unique individuals. Thus, after a period of time, generally two to five years after the inception of the marriage, couples often undergo soul-wrenching trauma. Unfortunately, personal growth is frequently slowed down rather than enhanced in early marriage. But although growth is painful, it is necessary for a healthier conscious dynamic between a man and woman; it is needed for a strong and flexible marriage. And it is difficult for people to confront and cope with such problems; they are hampered by defensiveness, ability to rationalize, and often a poor choice of professional assistance.

The women's liberation theme expresses this need to search for self-meaning. Yet the women's movement is only a help, not a substitute, for personal development. Everyone must search within for individual answers. Only in this development of self can both men and women survive the demands that marriage makes.

The need for ego-consciousness (self-identity) at the adult level is practically mandatory for the creation of a healthy marriage. Though unconscious needs or fulfillment of drives may at first seem enough of a foundation for a marriage, existence in today's world requires more substance. We are long past the primitive stage where the establishment of a family was merely an outgrowth of our sexual and procreative needs. Only those who come to marriage with a basic understanding and acceptance of themselves will be able to succeed over the long run.

Marriage provides, through imposition of socially created laws, a vehicle to fulfill the biological need to reproduce. It also provides a spiritual and practical economic framework within which we can function in today's world. It can signify continued growth if we come to it with open minds and a firmly established identity. It is a place from which we can engage life, sharing with another its blessings and burdens. It can make meaningful our passion, our pain, our goals, our need to be at once individuals and part of a larger picture.

Marriage provides the stage for making real what we consciously and unconsciously need to do: join with another to pursue the ultimate meaning of self and life. But only if we acknowledge and honestly deal with the forces that have made us what we are, and only if we continually try to achieve self-understanding in growth, can marriage be the vehicle for that sort of fulfillment.

II. The Attorney-Client Relationship

For too long it has been the accepted policy in dealing with matrimonial problems for the legal profession to concentrate only on facts related to finances and marital misconduct. The main emphasis has been on getting the history of family disunity for use in a matrimonial proceeding under the laws of the state in which the family lives.

Where state law designates various forms of misconduct, such as cruel and inhuman treatment, as a ground for divorce, a lawyer ordinarily tries to find incidents of the other spouse's conduct that fit the legal definition of such misconduct. The obvious effect of this approach is to reinforce the client's anger and discontent by having him or her recapitulate all the "dirty laundry" that has been accumulated during marriage.

Usually there is little if any discussion of the positive elements of the relationship, nor is the troubled spouse made to confront him- or herself with the possibility of searching for answers on a nonlegal level.

The lawyer's techniques are shaped by his professional training and also, of necessity, by the law in the state in which the case will be tried. Clearly, the nature of the law directly affects the structure of the family unit, the marital attitudes of the citizenry, and the approach of matrimonial lawyers.

As lawyer and client develop their case out of the external reasons for the matrimonial difficulties, there is a concomitant swing away from any understanding of any of the subsurface reasons. The lawyer sees his job as that of an adversary, coldly advocating the individual client's rights as they are set forth in statutes and legal precedents. The client is also led to concentrate on the specific legal aspects of his/her situation and to abandon any attempt at assessing the total family situation and his or her responsibilities within it.

No useful rethinking process or human progress can grow out of this procedure. The client is offered no opportunity to think about such factors as environmental conditioning, prior traumatic life experiences, past family life, current lifestyle, responsibilities at work, and pressures that exist as a result of those responsibilities, that may have played their subtle part in bringing him/her to this crisis. These and other factors can play a decisive role in weaving the particular fabric of a marriage. Whether the weave is strong or weak will depend upon the psychological structure and self-understanding of each of the individuals. Unfortunately, in the typical lawyer-client relationship, only the symptoms of a disturbed marriage are looked at—and not the disease itself. The individual client is thus prevented from achieving knowledge that could be helpful throughout the rest of his/her life.

There has to be a leap into this darker zone, and its contents cannot be fully understood without the assistance of allied medical professionals. Nor can it be understood unless lawyers themselves begin to approach matrimonial difficulties with a different outlook. To serve, one must understand. That service must of necessity be demanding. Lawyers who choose to practice in the marital area must meet these great demands, both educationally and humanly.

Of course, the typical matrimonial lawyer has problems of his own. For one thing, he must face economic reality, the need for skilled secretarial assistance, an appropriate office, and an adequate law library for research. With such pressures upon him, the attorney almost has to approach each case with an eye to charging a fee commensurate with real economic needs, and there must be a certain volume of cases each year if he is to stay in practice. Even if we view this same practitioner within the context of a larger law firm, the difference is negligible. In such firms the overhead factor is usually determined on a per capita basis whereby each attorney, whether partner or associate, must fulfill a certain minimum standard in terms of output. Often, year-end bonuses and salary raises in these types of firms are predicated upon the work product of the individual attorney and the amount of dollar productivity.

Thus attorneys may find little time for development of a case history that goes beyond the basic facts governed by the rules of law involved. No longer are they serving a public purpose but must consider their private interests too. Obviously, the practical financial and other pressures upon a professional person in metropolitan areas compound this difficulty, and alarmingly enough, it is in these very metropolitan areas that the divorce rates are staggering. In New York State alone there has been a 303 percent increase in divorce decrees from 1968 to 1973, with 11,331 decrees awarded in 1968 and 45,626 in 1973. What is even more staggering is that more than 50 percent of *all* civil actions filed in the Supreme Court were actions to terminate marriages.

These economic necessities directly affect the ability of the layman to obtain proper professional assistance. And in addition, the law itself can be a noose around the neck of a person who is seeking competent legal counsel. For the most part, women suffer far more than men, since in our economic structure men are more likely to have sufficient cash available to pay the legal fee for the "expert." Most attorneys who specialize in family law request an initial retainer of from $1,000 to $5,000. Even this may not be enough to cover the full costs of the legal representation. One can easily see that the law in regard to counsel fees and just who pays them becomes a pivotal question at the outset.

There are still many states in which the wife cannot request from the court, in advance or even during a negotiation, an amount to be paid to her attorney by her husband so that she can be represented by legal counsel equivalent to the specialist who will be representing his interests. For instance, in the state of New

York, there is no rule of law that would require a husband, who may have retained expert matrimonial counsel at perhaps a cost of $3,000 to $5,000, to provide the same amount to the wife so that she can retain equivalent expert help. It is only after a legal action is begun that the attorney for the wife has some degree of compensatory protection and may be awarded a fee by the court commensurate with the nature of the legal undertaking and his or her expertise. Even with that protection, attorneys are often reluctant to leave the amount of their fee to the discretion of the court.

In at least one judicial department of New York State, there is a rule of law that if the wife pays her attorney a counsel fee, even if she had to beg, borrow, or steal to obtain the fee, she is then without recourse in requesting reimbursement in the matrimonial action itself and is forced to institute a separate action at additional cost. At best, she would have to prove in the second action that the legal fee paid to her attorney was considered to be necessary and that the fee paid was fair and reasonable.

This inherent deficiency in the law creates a further impetus for the attorney who has not received a proper retainer to proceed as quickly as possible to a judicial confrontation. The angers and animosities between the spouses, which perhaps might be minimized by a more amicable, less hasty approach, are increased.

There has been much talk and media exposure of the notion that a matrimonial problem should preferably be handled by someone who has extensive litigation experience in this specialized area. To negotiate a fair and equitable agreement for a client, it may be necessary for the attorney to stand ready to back up the client's rights in the courtroom. But is this the key? Is this still the reality, given the knowledge we now have of the psychological and sociological factors that affect the marriage? Should the lawyer's readiness and ability to handle complicated divorce procedures in court be the only determining factor in the client's choice of a professional to represent her/his interests? What are those interests?

In many divorce cases it has been found that when all the dust settled and a divorce granted, there was an undercurrent of sadness to the severance of the marriage. One could say that this was merely a normal reaction to the destruction of a dream. But in psychological terms, the strength of the emotion seems to go far beyond this analysis. Evidence of this frequently emerges when a client undergoes supportive therapy or some form of psychological counseling after divorce. All too often it develops that the client's true needs were not at all touched upon in the course of the representation. In fact, the emotional factors that existed at the outset, combined with the snowballing effect that legal action can have upon them, may have forced the client to rationalize and defend against the possibility that the marriage was not dead and to be buried.

Perhaps 30 percent or more of the marriages that end in divorce might possibly be salvaged if there were a more enlightened approach by attorney and client. This would of course require the involvement of skilled allied professionals. Often, hasty decisions to divorce are made because of misconstrued anxieties and pain. With the proper counseling, some clarification of the problems would be offered early, growth could occur, and guilt would be minimized, whether the problem was finally resolved in reconciliation or divorce.

There are a number of cases in which clients, having dissolved the marriage and having subsequently sought some type of therapy, in due time remarried one another. Could not the pain of the divorce have been avoided altogether in many such cases if professional advice and assistance had been obtained *before* the divorce proceedings? Is it not possible that a caring and responsible attorney could guide many confused and unhappy couples to the therapist instead of to the courtroom?

Strengthening self-understanding and admitting past misunderstandings to oneself are well and good—but for a healthy marriage, this generally takes two, and often one spouse is unwilling. Would a lawyer's understanding and guidance to qualified professionals at the outset of divorce proceedings remedy this for some people? We believe that many couples might have reached a different perspective if more time had been taken to inquire into the causes of the rift in the marriage. There would have been more possibility of bridging the emotional gaps created during their difficult growth process as partners. And even if there could be no reconciliation, which is often the case, each person would have succeeded in gaining understandings that could have been the basis for a reasonable agreement in the parting of the ways, as well as a sound and healthy beginning to a new life as a divorced person.

What can the lawyer do for the client in this area of his need? The first thing, of course, would be to seek assistance from a professional person equipped either to deal with these human problems or to direct the client to an agency or individual that can deal with them. The trauma of a broken marriage can be the most severe psychological experience of a lifetime. It will affect all other aspects of the individual's current and future activities. Men and women must be encouraged to seek help that goes deeper than legal action—and often the attorney is the best, even the only, person to help couples see the need for deeper counsel.

The emotional, legal, societal, and financial pressures facing most matrimonial clients make them anxious, disturbed, and unhappy at the time they first consult a lawyer. At the same time, clients may also develop what one might call a healthy transference or identification with the attorney. The attorney can become a father figure or mother figure; or someone on whom to act out their inner angers and frustrations. The attorney can represent safety, wisdom, and security in the marital war. There is no question that the role of the attorney can be decisive to the client psychologically as well as legally. For this reason, both client and attorney must be aware of both the positive and negative possibilities of their relationship. The attorney in particular, because he or she is presumably not in a state of emotional crisis, and has been sought out for his/her services, is in a position of great responsibility.

Generally there is a certain image projected on the part of both the attorney and the client at the initial conference. Furthermore, the attorney, by virtue of his/ her training, will probably concentrate primarily on the legal aspects of the problem. It is important for the client to pierce this veil of professional competence and try to search out the attitudes and character of the attorney, the aspects of his or her make-up that will affect the entire nature of the representation. But it is also important that the lawyer try from the outset to assess the client's attitudes and needs, to see whether he/she feels compatible and competent in the situation.

Here are some useful questions the prospective matrimonial client should ask when "shopping" for a lawyer:

1. Has the attorney worked with allied professionals such as child psychiatrists, marriage counselors and adult psychiatrists, or other qualified medical professionals in representing marital clients?

2. What is the attorney's attitude toward efforts to effectuate some sort of temporary or permanent reconciliation, and to what extent will the attorney work toward that goal?

3. Does the attorney permit office conferences or telephone communication about the client's emotional state, and will the attorney work with a medical professional, if necessary, to understand the complexity of the marital problems?

4. What training or educational background has the attorney had in understanding the psychology of marriage?

5. Does the attorney interrupt the office conference with phone calls or other extraneous duties?

6. Will the attorney undertake to present his arrangement with the client in letter form, with respect

both to fees and services on behalf of the client and to the responsibilities each has to the other, including a partial refund of the initial retainer in the event there is a reconciliation or speedy settlement of the matter?

7. What is the attorney's attitude toward men and women? For the most part, because most matrimonial attorneys are men, the question arises as to their attitude toward women. Though the attorney may be able to detach himself from the subjectivity of the client, he may not be able to detach himself from his own conscious or unconscious predispositions.

8. What experience and background has the attorney in marital negotiations and in litigated matrimonial matters?

9. Does the attorney believe in extensive efforts at negotiation or will he insist upon going to court at once?

10. Does the attorney believe in conferences where husband and wife and respective counsel attend, including the possibility of having a medical professional present who is involved with the members of the family? (Often, such face-to-face meetings with the other side can help in piecing together elements that may have been hidden because of a client's guarded approach causing him/her to conceal the facts surrounding the marital history.)

11. Does the attorney clearly and succinctly outline the various financial, emotional, and legal implications at the initial conferences so that there is a clear picture of all possibilities for the client?

12. Does the attorney discuss other cases he has

handled with specific reference to names, fees, or other confidential information as a method of puffing up his self-image?

13. What is the instinctive feeling about the attorney after the initial office conference? Does a feeling of comfort and understanding exist? (The client must have that security and has a right to demand it or question its absence.)

14. Is the attorney open to honest comment or meaningful criticism? What is his reaction to questions or suggestions? In effect, does the attorney show a well-adjusted personality along with good technical ability?

15. Does the attorney respond fairly quickly to telephone calls, or is there an undue lapse of time? (Because the position of the attorney is so critical with respect to the client's emotional state, there must be immediate response, certainly no longer than twenty-four hours between call and return call.)

16. Is the attorney capable of dealing directly with the client's demands? (A client's anger and frustration may sometimes lead to unrealistic requests of the attorney and even to unsound suggestions about positions to be taken in the marital negotiation. The attorney must be prepared to confront the client and challenge unreasonable demands or rigidity.)

17. Does the attorney discuss with the client his acquaintance or friendship with various judges or with the attorney representing the other spouse? (Generally, this would be a bad sign, because the client's needs tend to reach beyond the legal area and the attorney may be, or seem to be, treating the client's problem casually

because of his confidence that such relationships will help solve it. This, of course, is detrimental to the careful and penetrating approach that is required. The superficial security of knowing "the other side" or "the judge" may lead to a lackadaisical attitude.)

This is by no means a complete list of the factors to be considered in choosing a lawyer. It is merely a yardstick which should help the prospective client measure the initial relationship with the attorney. No one answer is meant to signify an attorney's incompetence or lack of human understanding.

The psychological dynamic of a marriage must be considered relevant to the legal and social rules that apply to marriage. The attorney and the client must be prepared to delve into this area. Although a great deal of matrimonial law has not caught up with this principle, it is the responsibility of both client and the attorney to recognize it and use it properly. Without such awareness, people are likely to be viewed both by themselves and the legal system itself as automatons subject to principles of law which, though artfully conceived, fail to meet the real demands of the marital situation itself. Neither will they be encouraged to consider the complex human problems that lie below the surface of the marital conflict.

Our whole system of legal education creates a one-sided approach to the client. Those who have finished their course of professional study tend to feel fully educated. This is necessary. A lawyer must have this conscious conviction of his/her competence in order to survive in our society. Any doubt or feeling of uncertainty would undermine the confidence and authority necessary for a professional career. However, sadly, not all professional people *are* as totally competent and well-adjusted as they may feel or as they may appear to be. This creates a barrier to consideration of the essential element in most marital problems: What is the client's emotional state and how does it relate to the facts of the marital rift? How can an attorney, trained in a factual and logical approach to the law, search for these forces without feeling the very indecisiveness he is trained to avoid? After all, the legal structure itself calls for a presentation of the surface facts of the marriage relationship so that divorce, separation, custody, and property rights can be determined.

Thus many attorneys reject the help of medical professionals or other counselors or have a poor opinion of such experts. Asking for help can jar the ego and create grave doubts about the legal direction of a case. There is a high degree of intellectual defensiveness among lawyers vis-à-vis their clients. Their office desk itself bespeaks this silent fact. Distance is created as well as an often frightening image of authority. The defensiveness stems from a lack of understanding caused by an inherent defect in the educational process of the professional. Unconscious though this defense may be, it often precludes the most cherished of the rewards that an attorney can experience: human gratitude of the client and perhaps the soul-supporting feeling of having helped people to heal and grow.

Attorneys practicing in the domestic relations area cannot minister to a client's ills if they have not yet corrected faults within themselves. Their own attitudes toward themselves—their own psychological background and self-knowledge in relationship to the client's legal and human problems—is critical to the welfare of the client as well as to the family itself, which looms as the larger picture to be viewed in any legal representation.

III. Divorce

Divorce is the termination of the marriage relation and the marriage contract by direction of a court. Three other legal terms should be distinguished from divorce. *Annulment* is the invalidation of a marriage; i.e., a court declaration that the marriage never came into being, in contrast to divorce, which indicates that the marriage did exist, but has been ended by the court. *Legal separation* is a court determination that the marriage still exists, but that the parties are directed to live apart. *Dissolution* is a term used in some states as the equivalent of divorce; in other states, it is the equivalent of an annulment. However, in either case, the marriage relation is ended. In California, for example, under the recent law which makes "irreconcilable differences" or "irretrievable breakdown" the ground for ending a marriage, the word "dissolution" is used instead of "divorce." New York has four different categories of court judgments relating to marriage: divorce, annulment, separation, and dissolution. Dissolution in New York applies to the special case of marriages terminated on the ground that one party has been absent for more than five years without explanation, and the presumption that the party is dead. Popularly, this is known as the Enoch Arden law, and to some degree it was the forerunner of the "no-fault" divorce thinking.

Enoch Arden was the hero of a popular nineteenth-century novel; he was supposedly lost at sea and given up for dead. When he returned home to find his wife married to another, he nobly went off without letting her know he was still alive. Under the law as it existed then, the second marriage was void, and his wife was a bigamist. This led to clamor for a law that would protect the innocent spouse if one long believed to be dead turned up after many years.

The legal consequences of these four terms—*divorce, annulment, separation,* and *dissolution*—will be discussed in a later chapter.

GROUNDS FOR DIVORCE

In spite of the present trend toward liberalization of the divorce laws, the public policy of each state is still interested in the preservation of marriage. The party asking for a divorce must show good reason for his or her request. However, the quality and quantity of the

proof required varies from state to state—from very
little to very much.

No-Fault Divorce

In the past decade, more than half the states have
adopted a ground for divorce known variously as "irreconcilable differences," "irretrievable breakdown," or
"incompatibility." This ground is so close to being no
ground at all that it is referred to as "no-fault" divorce.

Each state has its own standard for the requirements needed to establish irreconcilable differences,
incompatibility, or breakdown. Some states require that
the parties show they have submitted to a reconciliation
procedure offered by the state. Others ask only for testimony that the parties have lived apart for a minimum
period, or that one or both of them feel they can no
longer live together.

New York State requires that the parties live apart
for more than one year under the terms of a written
agreement, acknowledged before a notary, and filed with
the court. In effect, this is a variation of the "no-fault"
rule.

Another variation found in New York, Alabama,
Hawaii, and Minnesota allows for divorce after the
couple has lived apart for a period of time under a court
judgment of separation. In New York, under the
Gleason rule, it does not matter that the separation
judgment was granted to the wife based on a finding of
fault against the husband. Jackie Gleason was granted a
divorce on the ground of living apart under his wife's

previously obtained judgment of separation based on a finding of fault on his part.

Fault Divorce

Divorce granted on a fault ground implies that one party is guilty of such conduct that the state recognizes that the marriage is dead, or that continued living together would be dangerous to the physical or mental health of the injured party.

Adultery

Historically, adultery was the only ground acceptable to the state for divorce. Adultery is voluntary sexual intercourse between one party to a marriage and anyone other than the lawful spouse. The definition of sexual intercourse has been broadened in many states to include "deviate sexual intercourse," which is further defined in the divorce law or in the criminal code of the state. Generally, it refers to homosexual conduct; sodomy in its various forms; and perhaps to some other acts in the infinite variety of sexual conduct.

Abandonment

Abandonment has three elements: simply leaving, leaving with intent not to return, and leaving without the consent of the other party.

Not every leave-taking is an abandonment. If, after

a bitter argument, the husband slams the door and yells, "I'm leaving, and I'm not coming back!" but he does come back in an hour, in a day, perhaps in a week, most judges would be reluctant to find that such conduct is a true abandonment. Suppose, meanwhile, the wife has changed the locks on the door and the husband is unable to re-enter. Under such circumstances, a judge might find that the wife's action and conduct is a "constructive abandonment" of the husband by—i.e., excluding him from the marital premises—and may be the equivalent of abandonment. But few cases will rest on such a bare recital of facts. The court looks at the whole picture—what came before and what went on afterward.

The intent not to return may be shown by evidence that he (or she) took his clothes, left word for mail to be forwarded, took up residence elsewhere, etc.

Abandonment, by definition, depends on lack of consent by the deserted spouse. In many instances in which there is a *bona fide* abandonment, the parties come together, sometimes in a lawyer's office, to enter into a written agreement to divide their property, provide for support for their children, etc. Many of the standard forms for such a separation agreement contain the phrase, ". . . the parties, having agreed to live separate and apart. . . ." Technically, the agreement to live separate and apart destroys the legal action for abandonment. Many judges will dismiss the action on the reasoning that a plaintiff cannot be abandoned if there is an agreement to live apart.

Parties often separate, come together again, and separate again until there is a final break. Suppose there has been an abandonment for more than the required time, and the parties attempt a reconciliation over the Christmas holidays while the loving spirit prevails but after a few days, they break up again. Does this mean that the abandonment has been forgiven and that the period of separation starts from the last parting? Everything depends on the circumstances, the length of time of the reconciliation, the wording of the law. In New York State, at least one judge thought the attempted Christmas reconciliation was commendable and should not prejudice the plaintiff if it failed.

Cruelty

Too often we project onto our spouse the flaw in our own soul and act it out as if we had no relationship to our own anger or frustration. Cruelty may be physical or mental; it may be by blows, or it may be verbal; it may be a course of conduct or a course of nonconduct. "Man's inhumanity to man" has many forms. In medieval England, a husband was privileged to beat his wife with a stick "no thicker than his thumb."

Times have changed. Pages and pages of examples could be offered to show what courts have accepted as "cruel and inhuman conduct" sufficient for granting a divorce. For example:

Shooting and wounding a spouse
Shooting at but not wounding a spouse
Hitting, slapping, kicking on numerous occasions

Threatening to hit, slap, kick, etc.

Refusing to have sexual relations

Insisting on having sexual relations

Insisting on having "unnatural" sexual relations

Boasting of having had sexual relations with others

Insisting that a third party live with the couple (the third party being the paramour)

Refusing to allow a third party to live with the couple (the third party being an in-law)

If a divorce is sought on the ground of cruelty in a state whose courts insist on real proof, it would seem necessary to engage a lawyer familiar with the practice in that particular state.

Drugs and Habitual Intoxication

Although about half the states consider these two grounds for divorce as separate categories, the other states classify them as forms of cruelty.

Accusations of drug abuse and drunkenness are very often linked with physical abuse. However, some states will accept a charge that the defendant is a habitual drunkard, or a drug addict, and has been for a period of years. Proof of arrest and conviction on such a charge would be sufficient.

Imprisonment

In many states, by statute, the confinement of the defendant in prison for a period of years is a ground for a judgment of divorce. There may be a question regarding this provision as to what is meant by a "period of years." Does the period start when the party is arrested? tried? convicted? or sentenced? Suppose the party has been released on bail and does not enter prison until after an appeal is decided against him? Suppose he is paroled before serving the complete sentence?

The confinement must be after the marriage; but what if the party was convicted before marriage and was not confined until after marriage? If the conviction had been concealed from the spouse, there would most likely be grounds for an annulment action.

These questions can be answered only by a careful reading of the words of the law, and by research to find what the courts of the state have done in the past when confronted with one of these problems.

Support

Historically, a husband had a duty to support his wife and family. Not so the wife. At common law in England, upon her marriage, title to everything a woman owned went to her husband; and therefore, he owed the duty to support her and their children. This is the root of the ruling in some states that only a wife may be awarded alimony, never a husband. Married women's property laws long ago ended a woman's inability to own property. But the one-way obligation to support still survives in a majority of the states.

Failure to support is regarded in some states as something less than the other grounds for divorce. In New York, for example, it is a ground for a separation action, and possibly a ground for an annulment action; but it is not a ground for divorce. However, in several other states failure to support is a ground for divorce.

Insanity

Insanity must be "legal insanity"—i.e., the spouse must have been found insane by a court, and usually must have been and still be confined to a mental institution. Mere irrational conduct would probably fall within the "cruelty" classification.

New York State terminates a marriage on the insanity ground by a judgment of "dissolution" of the marriage, which for practical purposes is virtually the same as a divorce. Precautions are taken to compel the plaintiff to share the burden of taking care of the defendant and preventing the insane party from becoming a public charge.

Marriage is also a "civil contract"; and a contract requires consent by persons capable of giving consent. An insane person is not capable of giving consent and therefore his or her contract is a nullity. Thus, if there was insanity at the time of entering the marriage, the marriage can be annulled.

Fraud

Fraud requires reliance by the plaintiff on a false statement made by the defendant which the defendant made knowing that it was false. The statement must be a material one such that if the plaintiff knew the truth, he or she would not have entered into the marriage. Fraud may also result from concealment of a material fact where there is a duty to speak out.

Marriage is a civil contract to which the regular rules for civil contracts apply. A civil contract can be set aside for fraud; and so can a marriage be set aside.

In those states which prefer to grant divorce rather than annulment for fraud, some of the following situations would be grounds for divorce:

Misrepresentation of Intention

Refusal to cohabit—i.e., refusal to have sexual intercourse
Refusal to have a religious ceremony
Refusal to support or set up a home

Physical Defects

Inability to have sexual intercourse
Pregnancy by someone other than plaintiff
Chronic, serious illness concealed from plaintiff

Concealment

Concealment of prior marriage, of prior divorce, of children

Concealment of drug addiction

Concealment of venereal disease

Concealment of homosexuality

In broad outline these grounds are the justification which the state will require before it grants a legal divorce. One must keep in mind that the quality of the proof of the acts varies from state to state and even from judge to judge. Only a specialist in the matrimonial law of a particular state can give an expert opinion on whether or not the facts of a particular case will stand up in court.

The following chart shows the grounds for divorce in each of the fifty states. "Incompatibility," "irreconcilable differences," and "irretrievable breakdown" are grouped together as *No-Fault*. Divorce based on separation agreement and separation judgment or separation are combined under *Separation*.

GROUNDS FOR DIVORCE*

	No-fault	Fault	Separation	Drug Addiction Intoxication	Insanity
Alabama	●	●	●	●	●
Alaska	●	●		●	●
Arizona	●				
Arkansas		●	●	●	
California	●				●
Colorado	●				
Connecticut	●	●	●	●	Dissolution
Delaware	●	●	●	●	●
District of Columbia		●	●		
Florida	●				●
Georgia	●	●		●	●
Hawaii	●	●	●		
Idaho	●	●	●	●	●
Illinois		●		●	
Indiana	●	●			●
Iowa	●				
Kansas	●	●		●	●
Kentucky	●				
Louisiana		●	●	●	
Maine	●	●		●	
Maryland		●	●		●
Massachusetts		●		●	
Michigan	●				
Minnesota	●	●	●	●	●
Mississippi		●		●	●
Missouri	●				

*There is presently pending in some states proposed changes in divorce law. This data, as above set forth, is complete as of July 1, 1975. It is suggested that local law be consulted to verify any change in the grounds.

GROUNDS FOR DIVORCE* *(cont.)*

	No-fault	Fault	Separation	Drug Addiction Intoxication	Insanity
Montana	•	•		•	•
Nebraska	•				
Nevada	•	•	•	•	•
New Hampshire	•	•	•	•	
New Jersey		•	•	•	•
New York		•	•		Dissolution
New Mexico	•	•		•	
North Carolina		•	•		
North Dakota	•	•		•	•
Ohio		•	•	•	
Oklahoma	•	•		•	•
Oregon	•				
Pennsylvania		•			•
Rhode Island		•	•	•	
South Carolina		•	•	•	
South Dakota		•		•	
Tennessee		•	•	•	
Texas	•	•	•		
Utah		•	•	•	•
Vermont		•	•		•
Virginia		•	•		
Washington	•				
West Virginia		•	•	•	
Wisconsin		•	•	•	•
Wyoming		•	•	•	

*There is presently pending in some states proposed changes in divorce law. This data, as above set forth, is complete as of July 1, 1975. It is suggested that local law be consulted to verify any change in the grounds.

IV. Children
and
Divorce

Our social structure stresses the importance of enjoying, nurturing, educating, and conditioning the child. Having children is still a sought-after goal for most men and women. A child becomes a vital addition to the life of the parents, bringing them the possibility of expanding their own self-concept through interrelationship with their offspring. A child can cause a spiritual rebirth; by the purity of love's demands he can offer the parents a human proof of their wholeness.

Yet the birth of a child can further aggravate any emotional disorder that may exist in a marriage, and the disorder may permanently affect the child's life in a manner that will in turn come to haunt the parents. It is the children of today's broken homes who will become the adults in tomorrow's marriages. Their future happiness is threatened by the forces that surround marital break-up today.

Called upon in most instances as the primary servant of the adult need, attorneys are nevertheless obligated to take their proper professional place in helping to solve the many family problems that arise in the pre- and post-divorce period with respect to the child. But are they responding to this obligation?

Our federal law specifically requires that every citizen have equal protection. Yet possibly the most forgotten segment of our society is the children. This situation has not arisen from lack of concern on the part of our legislators; but its roots lie in the judicial system itself. The mechanics of this system simply do not adequately deal with children and divorce.

First let us take the average case of divorce. Children cannot help but be involved. The client is directly helped by the lawyer to cope with the mechanics of this procedure. But there is little or no attention paid to the needs of the children involved. The parents, because so many of them are unable to deal with the causes of the marital failure and its subsequent emotional distress, tend to be defensive about their children's needs. Trained to believe that they must be perfect in their parental role, and unequipped to face their own problems, too many of them fail to perceive and attend to disturbances within their children. Thus it is the exceptional parent who provides counseling for the children in a pre-divorce situation.

It is clear that the need for a combination of professional skills in a working relationship with children of divorce is necessary; moreover, it is crucial to the future health of our society. We believe it is the attorney's responsibility to recognize this problem and do something about it. There is simply no one else at hand.

Almost unbelievably, most attorneys never even meet the children of their matrimonial clients. In fact most, if not all, custodial and visitation arrangements between the spouses are structured by the attorney at the suggestions of the husband and wife. It is rare that the children are consulted except in an instance when the parent is playing the tug and pull game of custody with the other spouse, and this kind of consultation has dangerous implications. The children, throughout the legal activities, are rarely truly represented. Their best interests are damaged by the subtle and harsh manipulations of the adults involved, and not fully provided for by the artful draftsmanship of the legal scholar.

The laws pertaining to children of divorce, although cast in an aura of good intent, have failed to bridge the gap between the legal and psychological realities of divorce as they pertain to children. This has been in part the result of the common working assumption on the part of most parents and legal professionals that everything will be satisfactory if the basic economic and legal difficulties can be worked out between the warring adults. And the theoretical approach that the courts act as quasi-parents to the children has failed simply because there is little time to undertake such responsibility. With overloaded court calendars, particularly in matrimonial cases (which make up on the average 50 percent of *all* legal work administered), less than minimal attention is given to children of divorce.

In the multiplicity of marital problems brought to attorneys it is most important that the emphasis should be in understanding the client's fears, angers, economic problems, human and legal expectations fostered and nurtured by the marital discord, together with *a clear understanding of the way these factors affect the children of the marriage.* Generally, the parents volunteer very little information about the children, unless there is an immediate tangible problem manifested in some overt conduct of a child. Yet we know that the emotional difficulties children labor with as a result of an unhappy home environment are acute. Only through probing the client and setting up, when necessary, a close working relationship with a qualified child psychologist or psychiatrist, can attorneys provide the children with their full rights as individuals.

Time and again it is found that the general tendency of adults who are proceeding with the burial of their marriage is to make allies of the children, both to buttress their self-image and to hurt the other spouse through alienation of the child. The destructive effect of such conduct shows itself in the continuing increase of marital breakdown in each adult generation since World War II, the increase among teenagers of drug abuse and delinquency, and the enormous number of parent-child abuse and neglect cases all over the country.

A close working relationship among medical and legal professionals in the pre- and post-divorce period with respect to children can forestall or prevent emotional difficulties which, if not treated early, will continue into adult life.

For the most part, divorce is accepted as a nasty experience for the entire family. As we have seen, professional help often should be sought in behalf of parents and children so that emotional, as well as legal needs are considered. There are additional ways, however, to protect family members involved in a marriage break-up. Because of the emotional problems of children and of each spouse before and during the severance, there must be safeguards built into the separation and divorce documents themselves. The method used should be equivalent to the needs expressed. In some cases, for instance, a tight custody and visitation article may be mandatory. Following is an example of such an agreement:

ARTICLE[1]

Custody

1. The Mother shall have custody of each Child.[2]

2. In view of the age of each child no special provision is hereby made with respect to the rights of the Father to have each child visit with him. The Father shall have such reasonable rights of visitation to establish an affectionate relationship between the Father and each Child, having regard to the interest and welfare of

[1]Reprinted with permission from PLI's 1975 course handbook *Matrimonial Matters* (Order No. F4 2782). Copyright © 1975 by Practicing Law Institute.
[2]The term "Child" refers to such Child with respect to whom an Emancipation Event has not occurred.

each of the Children and the maintenance of a similar relationship between the Mother and each Child.

3. The Child shall be with the Father for a reasonable period of time on Father's Day and on the birth date of the Father each year. The Child shall be with the Mother for a reasonable period of time on Mother's Day and on the birth date of the Mother each year. The Children shall be with both parents independently for a reasonable time on the birthday of each Child.

4. The Father shall call for the Child at the commencement of any visitation period, at the residence of the Child, and the Father shall return the Child to the Mother at said residence at the end of such visitation period.

5. The Father and the Mother shall promptly inform each other with respect to any illness or accident of the Child, and in the event that any such illness or accident causes the Child to be confined to bed or home (whether of the Mother or Father) for more than twenty-four hours, such other parent shall be entitled to visit the Child at reasonable times and for reasonable periods.

6. The Father and the Mother at all times shall inform each other with respect to the residence of the Child and the residence of each other and any removal of the residence of the Child.

7. The Father and the Mother at all times shall inform each other with respect to the physical whereabouts of the Child.

8. All the visitation periods of the Father are and shall be optional in all instances with the Father, nor

shall he be required to have visitation periods with all of the Children at the same time but same shall be at his option.

9. Each parent shall be entitled to complete and full information from any pediatrician, general physician, dentist, consultants or specialists attending the Child for any reason whatsoever, and to have copies of any reports given by them, or any of them, to a parent.

· 10. Each parent shall be entitled to complete and full information from any teacher or school giving instruction to the Child or which the Child may attend, and to have copies of a report given by them, or any of them, to a parent.

11. The parents agree to cooperate, and shall cooperate with respect to the Child so as, in a maximum degree, to advance the Child's health, emotional and physical well-being, and to give and afford the Child the affection of both parents and a sense of security. Neither parent will, directly or indirectly, influence the Child so as to prejudice the Child against the other parent. The parents will endeavor to guide the Child so as to promote the affectionate relationship between the Child and the Father and the Child and the Mother. The parties mutually will determine all matters relating to the health, education and general welfare of the Child, but in case of a disagreement as regards education, the Husband shall have the final decision. The parties will cooperate with each other in carrying out the provisions of this agreement for the Child's best interests. Whenever it seems necessary to adjust or vary or increase the

time allotted to either party or otherwise take action in regard to the Child, each of the parties will act for the best interests of the Child. Every reasonable effort will be exerted to maintain full access and unhampered contact between the Child and the respective parties. Neither party shall do anything which may estrange the other from the Child or injure the opinion of the Child as to the other party or which may hamper the free and natural development of the love of the Child for the other party.

12. The Child shall continue to be known by the name of the Father as set forth in the Recitals of this agreement, and by no other name during minority, and the name of the Child shall not be changed from said name, and the Child shall be enrolled in all schools and camps under said name.

13. In the event of the death of the Mother, the Father is to have the sole and exclusive custody of the Child.

14. The Child shall not be enrolled in any boarding school, college or university without the written consent of the Father.

15. The Father shall be previously consulted (unless such consultation is prevented by emergency) with respect to any hospitalization of the Child.

16. Neither party shall take the Child outside the United States of America without the consent of the other, which consent, however, shall not be unreasonably withheld.

17. Without the written consent of the Father, the

permanent residence of the Child shall not be more than fifty miles from the present residence of the Mother. A summer residence or vacation residence of the Child is deemed a temporary and not a permanent residence and accordingly, a summer or vacation residence of the Child may be beyond said area. In the event, however, that the Mother by reason of employment or remarriage is reasonably required to reside outside of said area and make the permanent residence of the Child outside said area and provided that such change of residence is not motivated by the desire or intent to render impractical or more burdensome the visitation rights of the Father, the Mother, if the Father after written request of the Mother shall not give such written consent, shall apply to a Justice of the Supreme Court of the State of New York, County of the residence of the Mother, in a proper proceeding, giving notice of such proceeding to the Father as directed by the Court and shall not so change the residence of the Child outside of said area until an order of the Court is obtained.

18. No breach or claimed breach or default of either party with respect to any term or provision of this Custody Article, shall affect or impair the rights and obligations of the parties under the other Articles of this agreement except that if the Mother violates the provisions of sub-paragraph 17 of this Article pertaining to the removal of the Children or Child outside of a radius of 50 miles from her current residence then the Father's support obligation as heretofore set forth in Article—— shall be temporarily discontinued until an adjudication is made by a Justice of the Supreme Court as hereinbefore set forth as to the issue of removal and visitation

or custody and the support and maintenance to be provided by the Father to the Mother and/or a Child.

In the recent matrimonial laws associated with child custody, we have seen a clear trend toward placing the greatest burden on mothers relating to custodial duties and responsibilities toward the child. Most legal rules bend heavily in this direction. Yet it was not so long ago that the men had an almost absolute right to custody of children! The common-law rule that governed this area until the nineteenth century regarded the father as the natural guardian of the children. This was generally based upon the fact that he was in control of all marital property and was vested with the legal responsibility to support the child. The emancipation of women in the nineteenth century brought with it changes in the surrounding marital law of custody and later on economic rights between husband and wife.

In time the law was changed to theoretically give both parents an equal footing to the legal right to custody in a marital dispute and to joint control of their children. However, from a practical point of view, the progress of decisional law thereafter turned more and more to the unwritten rule that the woman would retain physical custodial rights over the child. Exceptions were made predominantly on the basis of proof that the wife is unfit to assume full-time custodial duties.

Today change is taking place. Men are realizing more and more their own importance in the raising of their children. Moreover, they are seeking in many cases to receive the benefits and joys of parenthood. Men are increasingly asking for custody of their children. Meanwhile, women are expanding their own individual horizons so that motherhood becomes *one* of the necessary integral parts of their developmental process. But these changes are still in a preliminary stage. There is an emerging awareness of the vital need for a child to have substantive contact with both parents on a continuing basis. The following agreement shows one approach to these recent developments in understanding the child's needs in a divorce situation:

The parties have carefully weighed the question of the custody of the Child. In doing so, they have been guided solely by considerations touching upon the Child's welfare, based upon the close relationship and the love and affection that has existed between the Child and each of the respective parents. The parties agree that their main concern and indeed the most important area requiring a mutuality of action is to administer to the Child's needs and both parents in turn recognize the other's ability to administer to those needs. Based upon such considerations, it is agreed that current circumstance requires that the Father have physical custody of the Child and that he shall reside with him subject to the custodial rights and duties of the Mother and her specified visitation rights as hereinafter set forth. It is expressly agreed by and between the parties hereto that an atmosphere of flexibility shall prevail with respect to the joint custodial and visitation rights between the parties as they relate to the Child; that the Child shall have the ability to express his desires regarding visitation and/or activities to be planned by and between the parents for his benefit, and that at all times his best interest and welfare shall be of paramount concern to the Father and Mother.

In summary, it is clear that there are definite steps that can be taken to minimize the possible emotional damage to children of divorce:

1. There should be individual legal representation of children in any matrimonial proceeding to protect both their legal and their emotional rights.

2. Psychological examinations and/or counseling should be sought by the parents for themselves and for their children when necessary during a separation or divorce procedure. It is an attorney's responsibility to provide guidance in this area.

3. The emphasis in our society that has placed the burden of custodial supervision on mothers should be modified so that each parent has an equal responsibility for the healthy adjustment of their child.

4. In any marriage for which dissolution is considered, the parents should make a preliminary determination, with the help of qualified professionals, with respect to the grounds for dissolution so that children of the marriage can be protected in the event the claimed unhappiness between the parents is merely a momentary discord.

5. The concept of fault as the foundation for marital dissolution should be avoided and replaced with

the concept of irretrievable breakdown of the marriage so that if the dissolution of the marriage is a reality, the steps necessary to put it to rest can be minimized and in turn reduce emotional trauma to the adults and children involved.

6. There should be a close working relationship of legal, medical, and therapeutic professionals so that the legal and emotional rights of children will be safe-guarded before, during, and after a divorce.

The future of our society is founded upon the healthy development of today's children. Only when adults move to better understand themselves will they be equipped to recognize and ensure the rights of their children. In a separation or divorce situation, it is an attorney's responsibility to work toward these goals as well as toward the resolution of legal problems.

V. Separation

"Separation" is the catch-all legal term for the relationship of a married couple who live "separate and apart." They may live apart by direction of the court, in which case they are legally separated (*de jure*). Or they may live apart by agreement, which is called a *de facto* separation.

In early English law, there were two kinds of divorce. Divorce *a vinculo matrimonii* (from the bonds of marriage)—i.e., the parties were no longer married; and *a mensa et thoro* (from bed and board)—i.e., the parties were still married but no longer slept together. Today, a *mensa et thoro* judgment would be called a judgment of separation. We would say that the parties no longer "cohabit," meaning that they no longer have sexual relations with each other and, usually, that they no longer live in the same house or apartment. What is meant by living separate and apart pertains more to the sexual sense than physical living arrangements, however. The courts are well aware of modern living, and there are cases in which, if the living space is large enough, parties may live apart in the same house or apartment. But they cannot live "separate and apart" and continue to have sexual relations to be considered "separated."

A *legal separation* is a judgment of a court directing the parties to live separate and apart without terminating the marriage.

The marriage continues in existence with some inheritance and some tax benefits unaffected. Neither party can remarry; their status as married persons has not been altered. This is in contrast to dissolution, divorce, or annulment, all of which terminate the marriage. (Annulment, of course, means that the marriage never came into being.)

The separation judgment may provide for alimony, for custody, for child support, for division of property, etc. It may direct that one of the parties leave the marital home; but, conceivably, it could allow both parties to occupy the same premises provided that there was no cohabitation. For example, suppose a couple owned their home with adequate room for living. Suppose, also, the home contained the husband's office. To direct the wife and children to find other quarters would saddle the husband with unnecessary expense. To direct him to find another office would also be expensive and might have a disastrous effect on his business or practice. If there were no danger of violence because the parties might have daily contact, the court might very well allow the husband to keep his office while it directed him to find other sleeping accommodations.

There are at least three major reasons why people might prefer a legal separation to a divorce:

1. For some, divorce conflicts with religious principles. The parties should be advised, however, that a court-ordered separation, or even an agreement of separation, may become the ground for a divorce after a period of time. (See the Jackie Gleason case, discussed on pp. 26-27.)

2. A separation judgment leaves the parties still married so that for purposes of inheritance, widow's benefits such as Social Security, veteran's benefits, pension rights, and for some tax purposes, the parties' rights are not changed as they might be if the marriage were terminated by a divorce.

3. It may be easier to prove grounds for a separation than grounds for a divorce. Almost any ground, and any degree of evidence which would allow for divorce, would also allow for a judgment of separation (except separation by agreement). The converse is not true. For example, in some states failure to support is a ground for separation, but not for divorce. Abandonment must be for a period of one year for divorce (New York). No period of time is required for separation. Courts are less reluctant to grant separation judgments than they are to grant divorces because there is still a feeling in favor of the "sanctity of marriage." However, there are contrary attitudes. In Florida all dissolutions are divorces. There is no judgment of separation.

GROUNDS FOR A SEPARATION ACTION*

Adultery

Adultery is universally a ground for separation. New York State has now defined adultery as "the commission of an act of sexual or deviate sexual intercourse, voluntarily performed by the defendant, with a person other than the plaintiff after the marriage of plaintiff and defendant." "Deviate sexual intercourse" is defined in the Criminal Code and it relates to homosexual conduct, sodomy, and perhaps to other acts which the court may consider "unnatural."

Abandonment

For abandonment, the time requirement may be eliminated (New York), or the length of time of the abandonment may be less than is required for divorce. Refusal to cohabit (sexually) is considered "constructive abandonment" in some states.

Cruelty

Inasmuch as the courts do not consider separation to be as serious a social disruption as divorce, they seem willing to accept less convincing proof. Therefore,

*For definitions of most of these grounds, see Grounds for Divorce, pages 25-36.

refusal of sexual relations (constructive abandonment, above) may also be considered as cruelty.

Drugs and Habitual Intoxication

The courts are aware of the nationwide drug problem and proof of drug addiction is considered a ground for a judgment of separation under the heading of drug addiction or under the label of cruelty.

Imprisonment

Logically, it might seem that this ought not be a ground for separation, but it is. During the period of a defendant's imprisonment, the parties live apart, and the defendant's conduct while in jail can have no bearing on the desirability of enforcing living apart in the future. In claiming imprisonment as a ground for divorce, it is argued that the marriage has been dead for such a long period that the free party should be allowed to form a new marriage relationship with someone else. This is not a reason for granting a legal separation, however. It seems more likely that this ground for separation is meant as additional punishment for the criminal who commits a serious crime (felony) which results in lengthy confinement (three years in New York).

Separation by Agreement

Many couples who find they are incompatible live separate and apart by agreement (as distinguished from "by judgment"). This may be by a simple, informal oral agreement not to cohabit—i.e., no sex by mutual agreement. Or, with each party represented by a lawyer, they may have drawn up a written agreement which divides their property, provides for custody of children and support, visitation, etc.

As with a separation judgment, parties must realize that living apart for a period of years without reconciliation is a ground for divorce in many states (Alabama, Arkansas, Connecticut, Delaware, District of Columbia, Hawaii, Idaho, Louisiana, Maryland, Missouri, Nevada, New York, North Carolina, Ohio, Puerto Rico, South Carolina, Texas, Utah, Vermont, Virginia, West Virginia, Wisconsin, and Wyoming).

The magic words which distinguish abandonment from *de facto* separation are: ". . . the parties have agreed to live separate and apart." These words mean that abandonment cannot be used as a ground for divorce or separation. In fact, no separation judgment will be granted by a court if the parties have agreed to live separate and apart. They have made their own remedy, and they do not need the court unless the agreement is broken and they ask the court to enforce it. That would be a contract action rather than a matrimonial action.

Even though there has been abandonment, there may be an agreement. A husband who abandons his wife and children may meet with her in a lawyer's office and sign an agreement for custody, support, visitation, disposal of property, etc., *without* an agreement to live separate and apart. Such a course of action would not deprive the wife of the possibility of an action for abandonment.

Separation by Judgment

As we have said, a separation by judgment is one in which the court has directed the parties to live separate and apart without terminating the marriage.

A separation judgment may become the ground for divorce. Since the Jackie Gleason case in New York State in 1970, it has been recognized that the party whose fault was the ground for the separation judgment may, nevertheless, use the separation judgment as a basis for a divorce action. In the Gleason case, more than fourteen years had elapsed since Mrs. Gleason had been granted a decree of separation based on her husband's conduct. The conflicting arguments were as follows: on the one hand, this marriage was as dead as any marriage could ever be; on the other hand, Mrs. Gleason would lose her right of inheritance in what might eventually be a very substantial estate and that at the time she secured her separation there was no contemplation that the decree might ever be used as the ground for divorce. The argument prevailed that even a guilty party should be freed from a dead marriage. There were implications that Mrs. Gleason might be compensated for the possible loss of the right to inherit. And in 1974 New York passed a law to insure such compensation in cases where the "guilty" party used a separation judgment as the ground for a divorce.

Therefore, parties should be aware that living apart

pursuant to a judgment of separation carries with it the possible ground for divorce.

Separation Judgment Distinguished from an Order of Protection

In many states, the family court has the power to order one party to stay away from the other, or to stay away from the home. In most respects this is the equivalent of a judgment of separation. The family court may in the same order provide for custody and support for a wife and children; it may fix visitation privileges. Such an order has all the attributes of a separation judgment.

However, although a judgment of separation may be the ground for divorce, generally an order of protection may not be.

The reason for the distinction can be explained, but it cannot be defended logically. Historically, only the ecclesiastical courts had the right to deal with marriage. Much later, in England, the chancery (modern equity) court began to take over the suits for annulments, separations, and divorces. Divorces were, as we saw earlier, *a vinculo matrimonii* (from the bonds of marriage) or *a mensa et thoro* (from bed and board—what we now call "separation"). When the various state courts took over the administration of justice in the United States, those courts that inherited equity jurisdiction were generally called supreme or superior courts. Because the marriage relationship was considered so important to the state, the supreme and superior courts were given exclusive jurisdiction of annulment, separation, and divorce. Other courts, handling lesser cases, became known as inferior courts. In modern times, the distinctions have become less clear. Some states have one court for all judicial functions. Some states have created intermediate courts.

The family courts, where they are separate, are generally considered intermediate courts, not ranking with supreme or superior courts. Unless expressly provided otherwise by statute, only supreme and superior courts can issue judgments changing the marital status. The so-called inferior courts may, however, issue orders affecting but not changing the marital status (e.g., support, custody). Only judgment of divorce, separation, or annulment changes the marital status.

This is a hybrid situation that varies from state to state by statute. For example, New Jersey allows its family court to issue a protective order which it considers a judgment of separation. New York does not consider the protective order of its own family court to have the same effect as a judgment of separation, even though the order might have the same terms as the separation judgment. But New York, nevertheless, will accept a New Jersey family court order as a judgment of separation, and will grant a divorce based on living apart for more than one year pursuant to such an order.

VI. Annulment

A judgment of annulment is a declaration by the court that no valid marriage resulted from the marriage ceremony. Various grounds exist for a cause of action to annul the marriage, some seemingly similar to grounds for divorce or separation, but in some instances there is the requirement of corroboration by a third party witness in the proof required to obtain a judgment of annulment.

Until the recent expansion of the grounds for divorce, annulment was a favorite method of freeing the parties from their marital ties. Annulment puts the parties back into their status before marriage. They are free to marry again; they may satisfy religious scruples; and they avoid unpleasantness involved in getting and proving they have sufficient grounds for divorce.

GROUNDS FOR ANNULMENT

Non-Age

Marriage is a civil contract. Annulling a marriage because one (or both) of the partners is a minor is a special case of the general rule that "infants" (persons under 18 or under 21, depending on the state) may void their contracts. The law of New York State provides that the marriage clerk may issue a license if the man is between 16 and 18 years of age and the woman is between 14 and 18 years of age if there is written consent by both parents of the minor.

If a marriage between persons under age turns out badly, either party may apply for an annulment even though the parents had consented to the marriage. The court will generally look for some additional fact— cruelty, abandonment, failure to support—to justify the annulment. Only the under-age party has the right to bring the action; and the right is extinguished when the party continues to cohabit after reaching the age of consent. That age varies from state to state, and the local law controls.

Prior Subsisting Marriage

In this country, a person can be married to only one person at a time. If one of the parties to a marriage is still bound by a prior marriage, the second marriage is void. In such cases the court grants an annulment, or a declaratory judgment stating that the second marriage is void.

The action is simple if there is outright bigamy. But what of the party who rushes off to Haiti or the Dominican Republic and obtains a formal court paper saying the marriage is dissolved? Can that person re-marry?

The general rule is that if the procedure of the foreign court is strictly observed, and if one party actually was present and appeared before the court and the other party was represented by a duly authorized attorney who appeared before the court, then the divorce is good and will be honored in this country.

What of "quickie" divorces in this country? The "full faith and credit" clause of the United States Constitution requires each state to accept the valid judgment of a sister state. (Foreign country judgments *may* be accepted by a principle known as "comity"; i.e., we will accept their judgments if their laws are not repugnant to our social customs, but we are not bound to accept them.)

"Quickie" divorces are probably good if the court of the state which grants them has reasonable requirements (irreconcilable differences), a reasonable residence requirement (six weeks), and if the defendant has proper notice of the trial. When the parties are wealthy and there is apt to be a later contest for property, some unusual situations arise. Perhaps the most fantastic was the suit by one of the late Tommy Manville's wives to set aside his Nevada divorce. She claimed that it was her twin sister, not she, who went to Reno for six weeks to establish residence for divorce. She lost. In Rosenstiel, another *cause célèbre,* the wife charged that her husband had bribed the personnel of the Mexican court to change the records to show that a "bilateral" (both sides appeared) divorce was granted. If the divorce was void, then the subsequent marriage of the husband was void. She won.

Surprising as it may seem, if a party obtains an invalid divorce, remarries, and then sues for an annulment on the ground that the second marriage was void, the court may grant the annulment. Much depends on the facts of the case: whether the court feels that the bad conduct of the party bringing the suit is a bar to relief, or that a void marriage is a void marriage, and the court has no option. There are decisions both ways.

Proof may be difficult to obtain in bigamy cases. The bigamist can refuse to testify on the ground that bigamy is a crime and the facts may be incriminating. The other party to the first marriage can testify—if he or she can be found, and if he or she is willing. If not, the plaintiff is faced with proving a difficult negative: that there was a prior marriage may be easy to prove; but that the prior marriage is still in existence (i.e., that the other party to the prior marriage is not dead, that there has been no divorce or annulment in any other state or country) may be difficult to prove.

Fraud

The knowing concealment or misrepresentation of a material fact which induced the deceived party to enter into the marriage is fraud.

An action to annul a marriage may be based on concealment of a material fact where there is a duty to speak. There is no standard list of duties or of material facts. Only familiarity with the case law provides a guide to what is and what is not actionable.

Here are some examples of the kind of facts, the concealment of which entitles the other party to the marriage to obtain an annulment on the ground of fraud:

> Prior conviction of a felony
> Drug addiction
> A determination never to have children
> Knowledge of infection with a venereal disease
> Prior marriage(s) even when terminated
> Children by prior marriages
> Impotency

Misrepresentation is a common fraud. Before divorce became liberalized and annulment was a more usual method for terminating a marriage, there were several standard misrepresentation stories:

> *We came to my parents' house for dinner, and while we were there, he admired my nieces and nephews and said he wanted a big family. Later, after we were married, he admitted he said that so I would marry him. He admitted he never intended to have children.*
>
> *I told him we must have a church wedding.*

He agreed. Later, after we had the civil ceremony, he said he never intended to have a church wedding. He only said that to get me to marry him.

Other examples:

He said he had a well-paying occupation. He had—he was a thief.

He said he had never been in trouble with the law, but he had been convicted of rape.

She said she was a virgin, but she was the mother of an illegitimate child.

She said she was pregnant by the plaintiff, but she was not pregnant, and she knew it.

He said he was marrying for love, and that he intended to set up a home; but he used the marriage for immigration purposes and then left. (Time too short for abandonment.)

She said she had divorced her prior husband for cruelty; but he had divorced her for adultery.

These are but a few examples. The case books have examples covering every phase of marital relations.

SUMMATION

The marriage relationship may be terminated by annulment or divorce. Annulment terminates the marriage from its beginning. Divorce ends a marriage after the period it has been in existence.

Separation puts an end to cohabitation and living together on family terms. It leaves the marriage in existence in a kind of limbo.

VII. Property Rights of Husband and Wife

HISTORICAL BACKGROUND

The Common-Law System

According to common law, upon marriage, the husband obtained control of and a substantial ownership
interest in all personal property possessed by the wife.
The wife's interest in real property, such as a parcel of
real estate or a house, also passed to the husband by
virtue of a legally created marital right and she retained
only a right to support, a limited interest in his property
upon his death, and a right to a reversion of her property back to her also upon his death. In general she had
no legal claim to any property that was accumulated

during the marriage. These rules were drastically changed by the enactment of the Married Women's Property Acts.

Married Women's Property Acts

In the middle of the nineteenth century, in response to changing social conditions and increasing social and economic emancipation of women, legislation was passed in England and in most American state jurisdictions changing the legal status of married women. These laws were known as the Married Women's Property Acts. The laws were primarily concerned with correcting specific legal disabilities of married women at common law.

The Married Women's Property Acts established in legal theory that property brought into the marriage by a woman, as well as property or other economic rights subject to her control and power of distribution and obtained by her during the marriage, are regarded as her separate estate. In spite of all these benefits, neither the common-law rule nor the Married Women's Property Acts placed the husband and wife on an equal community of property footing.

Community Property

The system of community property that is in force in many states recognizes, for the most part, that marriage is an equal partnership. It does this by establishing a new class of property, called community property, consisting in essence of the assets or income received by the husband and wife during the marriage. This community property, in which each spouse has a legally defined interest, is normally managed by the husband subject to certain rules to assure the appropriate protection of the wife's co-interest. Each spouse continues to own or manage his or her separate property that is excluded from the community interest—such as gifts or bequests through death of a relative. Upon dissolution of the marriage by death of either spouse or divorce, each is entitled to his or her separate property plus one-half of the community property. This rule is subject to certain specific exceptions and qualifications in each of the states that have enacted this legal concept.

Modern Common-Law System

Since the enactment of the Married Women's Property Acts in those states that have retained the common-law rule, each spouse has an individual interest in his or her own property. Joint interests in property can be created by the manner in which property is purchased. Thus, if a private home is purchased in the names of the husband and wife, it is considered jointly owned. The same principle applies to other property, such as savings accounts that are in joint name. Each spouse can purchase property in individual name and dispose of it without obligation to the other. There is no community-property concept that applies to the assets accumulated in the marriage.

Equitable Property Distribution

In the majority of states today the courts, with certain variations considered, have the right to divide property accumulated during the marriage by both spouses upon divorce in an equitable manner based upon a variety of legal principles. In effect this system of property distribution combines both the community of property concept and the common-law rule by standards applied by the court to create a fair distribution of property. Title to any specific property is not controlling upon the court. Thus, if the marital home was purchased by the husband and placed in his name alone, the court could transfer the ownership rights to the wife if it saw fit to do so.

CURRENT MARITAL PROPERTY SYSTEMS IN THE UNITED STATES

Pure Common Law

Twelve states and the Virgin Islands continue to adjudge property rights between husband and wife according to the common-law tradition as revised by the Married Women's Property Acts. These states are: Alabama, Florida, Georgia, Maryland, Mississippi, New York, Pennsylvania, Rhode Island, South Carolina, Tennessee, West Virginia, Virginia, the Virgin Islands.*

*The above lists were compiled as of January 1, 1976 and may be subject to modification. New York State is expected to change its statute to create an equitable property situation in the fall of 1976.

Community Property

Eight states and Puerto Rico have enacted laws that apply the concept of a community of interests by the husband and wife in marital property. In general, the division is on a fifty-fifty basis. These states are: Arizona, California, Idaho, Louisiana, Nevada, New Mexico, Texas, Washington, Puerto Rico.*

Equitable Distribution Law

Thirty states and the District of Columbia allow for the distribution of marital property between the husband and wife in the equitable discretion of the court regardless of how title is held so as to effect economic justice between the parties. These states are: Alaska, Arkansas, Colorado, Connecticut, Delaware, District of Columbia, Hawaii, Illinois, Indiana, Iowa, Kansas, Kentucky, Maine, Massachusetts, Michigan, Minnesota, Missouri, Montana, Nebraska, New Hampshire, New Jersey, North Carolina, North Dakota, Ohio, Oklahoma, Oregon, South Dakota, Utah, Vermont, Wisconsin, Wyoming.*

DEBTS AFFECTING HUSBAND AND WIFE

Common-Law Rule

The rule applied before the passage of the Married Women's Property Acts was that a wife could not sue

*The above lists were compiled as of January 1, 1976 and may be subject to modification.

her husband on any contract he had entered into with her. Thus, if the wife had lent the husband $1,000 and received a legal promissory note from him during marriage, it was unenforceable by her.

Today's Rule

Subject to limited exclusions, in certain states, a wife or husband can contract freely with one another and if proper identification of a debt is established (usually a written document) there are available all the appropriate legal remedies to enforce payment of the debt, as for any other creditor.

In the event that John and Mary established a debt from him to her before marriage, the marriage event would not extinguish the obligation or render it void.

Generally speaking, there is no time limitation or statute of limitations in collecting a loan or other debt between husband and wife and, unless otherwise agreed between them, there is no interest chargeable as a matter of law.

Effect of Bankruptcy on Debts

Ordinary debts between husband and wife are dischargeable in bankruptcy, excluding the responsibility of the payment of support for either spouse and the child, if any. A debt between husband and wife can be converted into a support obligation, thus making it undischargeable in bankruptcy. Thus, if the husband owes $10,000 to the wife and they separate after executing a written agreement, if he agrees to pay this sum back to her in equal monthly installments of $80 for a period of more than ten years as support, it no longer constitutes payment of a simple debt but is construed as support and maintenance not dischargeable if the husband goes into bankruptcy.

Miscellaneous Considerations

Time for Repayment of Debt

It is the general rule that if a spouse agrees to sell property in order to repay a debt to the other spouse it must be within a reasonable period of time. This of course assumes that a specified period has not been set forth in a writing or by verbal agreement between the husband and wife.

Payment for Necessary Expenses

Necessary expenses are such items as food, clothing, medical costs, and similar day-to-day items of expense surrounding the standard of living of the husband and wife.

It has been held that any advances made by the wife or husband for use in paying ordinary family expenses while the couple is living together is not recoverable without an agreement between them for reimbursement.

Thus, if Mrs. Jones pays for food and cleaning expense for the household with money she withdraws from her personal savings account, she does not have a legal right to claim reimbursement from her husband unless an agreement exists between them.

Gifts by Family Members

It is the general rule that unless otherwise specified in an agreement, money given to a husband and wife or either by a third-party family member will be considered as a gift, thus abrogating the claim of any legal liability for repayment.

PERSONAL PROPERTY OF HUSBAND AND WIFE

General Principle Under Current Common Law

Subject to specific exceptions, the general rule in most jurisdictions is that a husband and wife may deal with each other as they choose with respect to real and personal property.

In community-property states either or both may consent to convert certain community assets into individually owned property. There should normally be a consideration exchanged for the transfer.

In common-law jurisdictions, if title to a car or any other item of personal property is purchased in the name of the husband or wife, then under normal circumstances it belongs solely to the named party.

Questions of Title and Ownership

The main criteria for division of personal property, separate from nonspecified personalty in community-property states, is determined by who owned the property before the marital difficulty. Marriage partners can own property individually, as joint tenants, tenants in common, or tenants by the entirety.

There are some general presumptions that are applied in the determination of title to personal property:

> 1. No *prima facie* right exists as to ownership; ownership will depend on the relevant facts.
>
> 2. Except for highly personal items such as wearing apparel, jewelry, etc., title to household goods must be proven by clear evidence of sale or gift.
>
> 3. There is a presumption that property purchased in joint name is owned jointly.
>
> 4. If a husband purchases goods in his wife's name there is a presumption that she holds title and a gift is implied.
>
> 5. Accumulation of funds in a joint savings account is presumed to be jointly owned even though either the husband or wife supplied all the funds.
>
> 6. For the most part, any or all of the legal presumptions creating ownership rights in personal property can be rebutted by either

of the spouses. This will normally require clear and convincing proof.

Gifts and Other Miscellaneous Rules

Below are some general rules applicable to personal property:

1. Where one spouse pays for personal property and takes title in the other spouse's name or in their joint name, a gift is generally presumed.

2. The mere fact of possession of personal property without more proof of the facts and circumstances as to how this came about raises no presumption as to ownership.

3. Where personal property is acquired with the husband's funds and is taken in joint names, it is presumed that a gift to the wife of a joint interest is intended.

4. Where a husband purchases or transfers property in the wife's name, a presumption arises that it was intended as a gift.

5. The general rule in establishing a gift is that there must be an intention to make a gift, delivery by the donor to the donee, acceptance of the gift by the donee, and that the gift must be final and irrevocable.

6. The expressed intent by either spouse to make a gift to the other in the future will not

give rise to an obligation that the law could enforce.

7. The burden of proof in establishing a gift is on the party who claims it.

8. Household goods, furniture, and furnishings acquired by the husband or wife or both for their mutual use and benefit is generally considered to belong to both of them jointly. If there is no agreement upon a division of the household goods, furniture, and furnishings, the property will be ordered sold by a court and the proceeds equally divided.

9. Where a person deposits his own money in an account in his name and another's, this will ordinarily create the equivalent of a tenancy in common. If the depositor and the other named interested party are husband and wife they may establish a tenancy by the entirety.

10. The establishment of a bank account in the name of the depositor "or" another raises a presumption of intent that the balance on hand upon the death of either should become the absolute property of the other. This is, however, subject to rebuttal.

Wedding Presents

The general rule applied to gifts made to a husband and wife is that whatever the nature, except personal items or those gifts clearly earmarked for either, if they were intended for common use in the marital household then they are the joint property of both parties to the marriage. This rule should likewise apply to purchases of personal property for the household made from cash wedding gifts.

TYPES OF JOINT OWNERSHIP BETWEEN HUSBAND AND WIFE

The following categories of ownership are most frequently found to exist in the practical economic realm between a husband and wife. The significance of each type of tenancy, as it is called, revolves around the nature of each spouse's interest in the property in question and what becomes of that interest upon divorce or death.

Joint Tenancy

Joint tenancy can be created in real or personal property and arises by purchase or grant to two people (for our purposes here, husband and wife). Each has an equal interest and owns an undivided share equal to that of the other. The essential distinction of this type of tenancy is the right of survivorship, by which the entire tenancy on the demise of the other joint tenant evolves, by law, to the survivor.

Thus, if husband and wife open a savings bank account containing $1,000 in joint name, they each own an undivided one-half interest. If the husband dies, the wife is entitled to the whole balance. If the parties are divorced, each is entitled to $500. If the husband or wife withdraw without permission more than one-half of the balance in the savings account, then the other spouse has a claim for the amount over and above the other spouse's one-half interest.

Tenancy by the Entirety

A tenancy by the entirety is a form of ownership in which husband and wife jointly own real or personal property; when one of them dies the survivor takes title automatically, just as if the property were in joint tenancy. However, a creditor would not be able to seize a debtor's share of the property, as would be possible in joint tenancy; in tenancy by the entirety a creditor would have to secure a judgment against both husband and wife in order to seize such property. The legal implications of tenancy by the entirety apply only to transfers on purchases by a husband and wife. The general rule is that a transfer of ownership of property to a husband and wife automatically creates a tenancy by the entirety unless specifically stated otherwise. Thus, a deed for the purchase of a home sold by John Jones to Mary *and* Frank Smith creates a tenancy by the entirety.

This form of tenancy can be terminated only by the joint action of husband and wife during their lives, whereas a joint tenancy may be terminated by the sale or gift of one tenant's interest to the other. A tenancy by the entirety terminates if the husband and wife divorce—the parties then become tenants in common (see the next section).

Thus, if husband and wife purchase a home, as above, and thereafter separate from each other, it would be practically impossible for either to effectively sell his or her interest in the home to a third party. One practical reason is that the third party gets nothing more than the interest that was sold. Because this interest is subject to the survivorship right in the event the spouse who conveyed his interest died before the other, then the third party would be left with no rights to the home for the surviving spouse would take the whole.

Tenancy in Common

A tenancy in common exists when property, either real or personal, is owned jointly by the husband and wife; but in this case where one of them dies, his or her share is *not* inherited by the other owner but goes to those designated in his or her will. Because of the absence of survivorship rights, the equal share of each spouse may be freely sold.

Community Property and Personalty

The general rule surrounding a spouse's interest in personal property where the concept of community property applies is that each spouse has an undivided one-half interest in the whole. This may be likened to a partnership of equals. Each spouse may convey by sale, transfer, or otherwise his or her interest to the other during the marriage. Divorce generally converts community property into a tenancy in common, in which each has a one-half interest in the property.

Notwithstanding the general principles referred to above, property can be acquired by either spouse as their separate property. The rules surrounding gifts and bequests of property, etc., listed before on pages 77-81 are generally applicable.

EXAMPLES OF SETTLEMENT OF PROPERTY RIGHTS BETWEEN HUSBAND AND WIFE IN THE EVENT OF DIVORCE

Mr. Jones has been the sole wage earner in a marriage of eighteen years. He has bought a private home with a market value of $75,000 and a family car, both in his name. The Joneses have, at the time they seek a divorce, two children, ages 11 and 14.

Common Law

Under the property law relating to those states that apply the common-law rule, Mrs. Jones would have no interest in the house or the car. She and the children would conceivably be given the right to occupy the house, but this too is an open question if Mr. Jones decides to sell it.

Community Property

In those states that apply the community-property concept, the court would have the abso-

lute right to divide the value of the house and car between Mr. and Mrs. Jones. Thus, the mere fact that title to these two items was taken in Mr. Jones' name is not binding—the marriage is viewed as a partnership of co-equals. (There are minor exceptions to this rule, such as in a case in which the wife is guilty of marital misconduct. This is discussed in another chapter.)

Equitable Distribution

In states that apply the equitable distribu-tion concept, the allocation between Mr. and Mrs. Jones could conceivably be the same as in a community-property jurisdiction. Again, title is not a determining factor in the court's decision. Furthermore, it is possible that the court could award Mrs. Jones the ownership of the house if circumstances warrant.

The theoretical approach in the states that apply the equitable distribution principle and the community-property states is that the courts recog-nize the contributions made by a wife as housewife and mother, whereas in the common-law states the wife's contribution in these vital areas is not considered in the distribution of property.

In 1947, when Frank and Carmela married, Carmela had a savings account containing $25,000. She advanced the entire sum to help Frank start his business and worked with him throughout the first five years of the marriage helping him to make it a viable operation. Thereafter, two children were *born and Carmela continued to help in the business by entertaining business clients from time to time at their home. The business was placed in Frank's individual name and the home they lived in was purchased by them as tenants by the entirety. After twenty-five years of marriage, Frank fell in love with another woman and abandoned Carmela.*

Common Law

Under the property law of a common-law state, Carmela has no absolute right to share in the value of the business. It might be possible for her to claim some equitable ownership in the business, but it is a most difficult procedure. Furthermore, it will probably be presumed that her $25,000 was a gift to Frank unless there is a written document stating that it is a debt owed to her by the business or by her husband. Furthermore, Carmela cannot claim any sums of money for the labor and services she has contributed. The house, under the law of these states, will be converted to a tenancy in common upon the occurrence of a divorce and both husband and wife will each have a one-half interest upon the eventual sale.

Community Property

Under the law of states that apply the community-property concept, Carmela is entitled to one-half of the value of her husband's business in addition to one-half of the value of the house.

Equitable Distribution

In states that apply the equitable distribution concept, the court has more flexibility in assessing the equitable interest of husband and wife in both the business and the house. Thus, the court could award Carmela ownership of the entire house as a way of equalizing the distribution of property between the parties. If the business is valued far in excess of the house, then the court could award some form of cash payment over a period of years to create an equitable balance between the parties.

VIII. A Guide to Separation Agreements and Property Settlements

A separation agreement, sometimes called a property settlement, is an attempt by the parties to, fix their duties and obligations to each other for the foreseeable future. They negotiate with each other, hopefully through their lawyers, to put into words what each wants and what each is willing to do.

When there is bitterness, as so often is the case, the tendency is to drive a hard bargain. If the bargain is too hard to live with, the future will harvest further legal and possibly severe emotional trauma.

When civilized people reach the point where they know their marriage must be dissolved, agreement is the practical way to work out guidelines for custody, visitation, alimony, support for children, and division of property. It is an old axiom in the legal profession that an agreement is always better than a court-ordered disposition. No court has the time, nor can it afford the patience necessary, to achieve a result as good as a good negotiated settlement. As mentioned in previous chapters, professional counseling often can help to minimize marital war between the spouses.

Although negotiation is the best means to resolve conflicts between the parties, it is not without pitfalls; for it presupposes that five, ten, twenty years into the future, the solutions that are crystallized in the agreement will still be fair. Agreements that provide for periodic future review are rare. Obviously, at some future time, parties with great present earning potential may have become destitute. Healthy people may become ill. The woman or man who was determined never to marry again has had a change of heart. Inflation, in the past few years, has turned what were once generous settlements into pittances. Changes in the tax structure may turn a fair share of increased earnings into an intolerable burden.

Essentially, a separation agreement is a gamble. When parties gamble with each other, very seldom do both parties win.

AGREEMENT AS A CONTRACT

A separation agreement, or property settlement, is also a civil contract to which most of the rules for civil contracts apply. Like other civil contracts, it is based on mutual promises—i.e., the husband promises to pay alimony in return for which the wife promises to relinquish rights; the father promises to pay support for the children and the mother promises to care for them and allow visitation. This, of course, is a simplification because the agreement is more complex and does not pit one promise specifically against the other. It might, but usually it does not.

Although a separation agreement is a contract that is in many respects the same as any other contract, it is, nevertheless, different. The state has an interest it does not have in other contracts. This is an agreement that may lead to the dissolution of a marriage, and the state has an interest in maintaining all marriages. This is an agreement that may affect the welfare of children, and the state puts the welfare of children above the interests of the mother and father.

Therefore, certain things are special to separation agreements. No arrangement for custody or support of the children is permanently binding. Whenever there is a showing of a substantial change of circumstances, the state will allow the agreement to be changed regarding child support, visitation, and custody. This is not true of business contracts. If you can't pay the installments on the car because you lost your job, you cannot ask the court to change your contract.

Another provision peculiar to matrimonial contracts is an agreement to obtain a divorce. This is a gray area rather than a black and white situation. The state has two conflicting interests: to preserve all marriages, and to free parties from dead marriages. Thus, in most states it has long been the law that one cannot make a contract to buy a divorce. However, there are times when there is only a subtle difference between a contract made to induce a husband or wife to sue for divorce and a contract to settle financial and family problems in which both parties contemplate divorce. The twistings and turnings of the courts when they are confronted with this problem varies from state to state.

A leading case in New York State, *Butler* v. *Marcus,* (1934) 264 New York 519, holds that the contract may provide that if the parties are still married at some future date, the contract becomes inoperative and whatever has been paid or transferred must be returned. Obviously, the husband (or wife) has said, "I'll give you so much if you consent to a divorce by such and such a date." If either party used such language in the agreement—i.e., "I will pay you to get a divorce"—New York would say the contract is void from the beginning. Many other states look with suspicion on any separation agreement that is tainted with an inducement to obtain a divorce, and will refuse to enforce such an agreement.

This refusal to enforce separation agreements must be balanced against the reasons for enforcing them. It is good for the parties to know where they stand. A lawyer should be able to tell a client with some finality that this is his or her obligation, and that the terms cannot be changed by some later application to the courts. Also, the courts have an interest in encouraging the parties to agree without a trial because the agreement relieves the court of the burden of hearing a mass of evidence to decide what is right for the parties. If the parties agree that their contract is fair, they avoid the risk of a harsh decision rendered by a judge who may not be able to spend the time to explore the possibilities as thoroughly as will two competent opposing lawyers.

INCORPORATION OF THE AGREEMENT IN THE DIVORCE

As was discussed in Chapter III, the separation agreement itself may be the ground for divorce. Living apart for a period of years pursuant to an agreement can lead to divorce in almost half the states. What happens to the agreement when the court issues a judgment of divorce?

There are three possibilities:

1. The agreement may become merged in the divorce judgment—i.e., some, or all, of its terms are made part of the judgment. In the absence of some affirmative statement that the agreement is to survive as a contract, the agreement is extinguished by the judgment.

2. The judgment may say that the agreement is incorporated and shall survive the judgment—i.e., the terms of the agreement have become part of the divorce judgment; but the agreement as a contract lives on separate from the judgment.

3. The judgment may say (or the agreement may say) that the agreement is not part of the judgment, but nevertheless, the agreement survives the judgment as a contract between the parties.

The difference between these possibilities is that

1. If the agreement is extinguished, only the judgment controls the rights and obligations of the parties. This is of major importance when it comes to enforcement.

2. If the agreement is incorporated with the provision that it survive, then the parties have the option of the procedures for enforcing divorce judgments as well as the different procedures for enforcing contract rights and judgments.

3. If the agreement is not incorporated but, nevertheless survives, then the parties (as in #2 above) have the option of either divorce or contract enforcement; but the terms of the divorce judgment may not necessarily be identical with the terms of the contract, and the results may be quite different. The court has no power to change the terms of the contract (except for children's rights). But the court usually has a statutory right to change the terms of the divorce.

ENFORCEMENT OF THE AGREEMENT OR PROPERTY SETTLEMENT*

A divorce judgment, as distinguished from the obligations fixed by a contract, is a direction to the

*The entire subject of enforcement is taken up in greater detail in Chapter XI.

parties to do certain acts—to pay alimony and/or support, to allow visitation, to transfer property. Wilful failure to perform an act directed by the court is contempt of court. The court may also impose a fine for the amount of arrears or alimony and support with a direction that the fine be paid directly to the wife. The punishment for contempt of court is imprisonment for a limited time or until the act is performed (Chapter XI).

A judgment for breach of contract is a different matter. Failure to pay the amounts agreed upon in the contract results in a judgment for money. In such a procedure the sheriff is instructed to find property of the defendant, seize it, sell it, and turn the proceeds over to the plaintiff to satisfy the judgment. But if there is no property there are no proceeds. In this case the guilty party becomes "judgment-proof." Very few people are truly judgment-proof. Usually, they have salary, trust income, stock market accounts, pensions, or other funds that can be taken or "garnished" to satisfy the judgment. Both the collection and the avoidance of judgments is a vast subject that can only be touched on here.

Why bother with a contract at all? The answer is that a contract has more permanence than a judgment of the court. The United States Constitution and business practice prevent the courts from changing the terms of a valid contract no matter what change of circumstances the parties have undergone. If the contract provides $100 per week, the court cannot direct the payment of more or less in a suit based on a contract. This is not true of a judgment of the court—what the court has done it can undo. If the parties cannot meet the terms of the divorce judgment, the court, for good cause shown, can raise or lower the alimony and support, or forgive payment entirely.

This situation—immutable contract, changeable judgment—is not quite as absolute as it might seem to be. If the parties have made a bad bargain, generally they must live with it. However, some bargains (contracts) have become so bad with the passage of time that the court may feel it necessary to override the sanctity of the contract law. This is why it is said that marriage contracts are not quite the same as business contracts.

Perhaps the most usual, if not the saddest, cases arise from divorce judgments with a surviving contract that requires the husband to pay alimony and support at what is, at the time, considered a reasonable rate. If, years later, the husband remarries and has a second family, he cannot reduce support for the first family— the contract will not let him. Thus he may not be able to adequately support his second family. As a recent New York decision stated, "The public harm resulting from the destruction of the second marriage by economic strangulation is worse than tempering the husband's obligations so that he may work to full capacity with some incentive to meet these obligations."

There is a trend to find ways to avoid the strict construction of the contract terms and to allow the court to make adjustments by changing the divorce judgment. The state of Florida, for example, has declared by statute that the court has a right to modify, thus adding an unwritten clause to every separation agreement giving the court such power. A state may pass a law that denies to a party the right to enforce a provision of the contract which that state feels is contrary to public policy. New York State will not enforce a contract provision that declares that a wife is to receive no alimony; neither will it allow a lump-sum payment, which is all too easily squandered, in the event the wife seeks support or alimony thereafter. The aim is to prevent shifting the burden of support to the state.*

CONTENTS OF THE SEPARATION AGREEMENT

To some extent, each agreement is unique to the situation and the peculiar needs of the parties. There are general provisions and special provisions, which can be tailored to the individuals' specifications. Expert legal advice can be of great benefit.

Recitals

Every agreement should begin with statements that set the stage and locate the parties in time and place. It is a good idea to have an index which would make it easy to find the subject matter.

Date

The date of the agreement is important; it gives the point of departure for the assumption of duties and obligations. The date of the agreement may not be the date that alimony or visitation begins; but it marks the

*Legislation is now pending to change this rule in New York State.

date before which these provisions cannot begin as contract rights. If the agreement is to be used later as the basis of a divorce for "living apart pursuant to an agreement," then the date of the agreement marks the beginning of the running of the period—unless the contract must be signed before a notary, in which case the date of notarization controls.

Names of Parties and Children

This requirement is obvious. What is often omitted inadvertently is the birth dates of the children. The birth dates are important to fix the date when the children reach their majority and are no longer covered by the duty to support.

Residence of Parties

The residence of the parties should be set forth in the agreement as well as the place where the agreement was made. In the absence of a statement that the agreement is to be interpreted by the law of a specific state, the place of execution of the agreement and the residence of the parties would control.

Time and Place of Marriage

This provides the acknowledgment that there is a valid and subsisting marriage.

Real and Personal Property

Real estate that is to be affected should be described in detail. Personal property, which will consist of a list of items, may be placed in an appendix of the agreement.

Consideration

"Consideration" is a word with a special meaning in the law of contracts. In the context of a separation agreement, it means, roughly, "what is given for what." A promise to do something a party was not already obligated to do, in return for a similar promise by the other party, is "consideration." A transfer of real estate or personal property is "consideration." To denote consideration, lawyers use a phrase which the courts hold sufficient. The magic words are, "For $1 and other valuable considerations . . ." Without consideration, no contract is binding. The phrase appears in virtually every agreement prepared by lawyers as a safeguard in case one or more of the promises or acts exchanged should prove to be illusory.

Right to Live Separate and Apart

Neither party has the right to live separate and apart as a matter of law. Each has the right to demand that the other cohabit with him/her. Giving up this right—i.e., agreeing to live separate and apart—could be enough to satisfy the mutual promises necessary for "consideration" to make this kind of agreement a binding contract. (Note: If the parties agree to live separate and apart, neither party can claim abandonment as a ground for divorce or separation. Legally, one cannot agree to be abandoned.)

PROVISIONS OF A SEPARATION AGREEMENT

Separation

A brief statement is required that the parties are living apart and that they intend to continue living apart without interference by one or the other. If the parties are engaged in a joint business, they ought to provide that one may continue the business or profession and that the other may compete if a new business or profession is to be established.

Debts

There should be a statement about outstanding debt, business or personal. There is a well-known marital conflict syndrome—when either party decides a split is inevitable, that party tries to corner the marital assets. The wife may run up big bills on her charge accounts; the husband may mortgage everything owned in his name. Generally, in the agreement, the wife agrees that she has no outstanding debts beyond a certain sum, and that there will be no liability on the part of her husband for her debts incurred after the date of the agreement. There is no reason why the husband should not make the same promise to the wife.

Personal Property

There are usually lists of personal effects appended to the agreement. One list might include all the personal property the wife is to keep; another might enumerate all the personal property the husband is to keep.

Often, parties simplify this provision by a statement such as, "The wife shall remain in the marital premises and shall have title to all personal property therein, except [list], which shall belong to the husband.

What is personal property? Anything that is not real property. What is real property? Land, houses, anything attached to the land or buildings on it that cannot be removed without damaging the land or buildings. This is a workable definition a lawyer might want to expand. The new heating plant installed in the house is real property; the new washing machine connected to the plumbing may not be. The pictures hanging on the wall are personal property; but the murals painted on the wall may not be.

Real Property

Provisions for the disposition of real property ought to be written by a lawyer. Real estate has been the subject of bitterly contested suits for so many hundreds of years that the law is extremely complicated, even though it might not seem to be. Therefore we will briefly describe tenancy by the entirety and joint tenancy again. (See also Chapter VII, pp. 81-83.)

Tenancy by the Entirety

This is the legal term for the ownership of property by a married couple. Originally, it applied only to real

estate, but some states now use the term for the ownership of personal property as well.

Tenancy by the entirety means that the husband
and wife together own the whole of the property and
that when one dies, the other gets all. When tenants by
the entirety divorce, their ownership of property
becomes a *tenancy in common* (see p. 83) and either is
entitled to force a sale, if necessary, to collect half.
Tenants by the entirety must sell their property together; one cannot act without the other.

Joint Tenancy

Banks usually describe husband and wife accounts
as joint tenancies. Stocks held by a married couple are
usually held by them as joint tenants. This description
insures that if one spouse dies, the other automatically
becomes the sole owner of the property. But, if there is
a divorce, the parties may insist that the property be
divided "as their interests may appear"; i.e., if, for
example, the wife can prove that all of the money in the
joint bank account or all the money for the purchase of
the stock came from her earnings, she will probably be
declared sole owner.

Custody

If there is a divorce, the judgment will provide that
either the father or mother is to have custody of the
children of the marriage. Sometimes, as a face-saving
device, the court will award joint custody. The same
possibilities can be taken care of in the agreement. The

test, if any, is: which parent will best serve the needs of the child? Conceivably their time could be divided so equally that there is no appreciable difference. This seldom is the case. Although there is no general rule, courts generally hold that very young children (up to about 6 years) should live with the mother. Beyond that age, taking all circumstances into consideration, the courts are tending more and more to place boys with their fathers and girls with their mothers. At about age 15, give or take a year, the child's wishes will have great weight; for a child of that age is thought to have rights in the choice of where he/she will live.

Custody provisions should set forth the address of the child's home, arrangements for notification in case of accident or illness, and details regarding consultation for schooling and religious instruction. A recurring problem, with many different solutions, is what to do when the child's home is moved—to another state, or even another country.

Visitation

Visitation is one of the most delicate areas of a separation agreement. Friction can be avoided if the time, the place, the duration, and all other conditions for visitation are set forth in the agreement as explicitly as possible. Provisions should be made for holidays, holy days, school recess, vacations, Mother's Day and birthday, Father's Day and birthday, and any other days special to the parties. Provision should also be made for the time and manner of notification if either party must cancel visitation. Spelling out details like this in the agreement reduces the chances that the child will be damaged by the emotional consequences of a parent not showing up or one parent attempting to use the child to hurt the other (see Chapter IV).

Child Support

The amount of child support is a matter for each particular case. There is no universal rule. The elements to consider are: the mother's earnings, the father's earnings, the number of children, the previous standard of living, the physical health of the child, its age, the need to provide for health insurance and life insurance to give permanent security in case a parent dies. Child support is nontaxable to the recipient parent.

Who will pay for the child's education? Should there be private schools and college? Will the parents consult and choose a school by mutual agreement?

If there is serious illness, who will choose and who will pay for the doctor? the hospital? Everything related to these eventualities should be spelled out in the separation agreement.

Child support generally ends upon the emancipation of the child—i.e., the child's attaining the age of 21 (lower in some states), marriage, becoming self-supporting, entering into military service. There is no law to prevent support of a child past its majority or emancipation, although this is seldom done except in cases of incompetent or severely handicapped children.

Sometimes provision is made to continue support past age 21 for a child in college or graduate school. One father who had agreed to such a provision withheld support when he found that his daughter had left the college dormitory and was living off campus. The court upheld him, because if he was to continue support he had the right to decide where his daughter should live.

No matter what agreement the parents make, the court is not bound by it. Upon a proper showing, the court may at any time order a change of custody and a change of support.

Is the right to visitation dependent upon payment of support? Yes, if the court so states in the judgment. Yes, generally, if support and visitation provisions are dependent in the separation agreement. No, generally, if there is no agreement and the court's direction in the judgment does not tie visitation to payment of child support. The theory in the latter case is that if a party does not comply with the court's direction, the remedy is to apply to the court to punish the offender for contempt instead of withholding visitation to force payment.

Alimony

Books have been written devoted solely to the subject of alimony. Only the highlights are presented here.

Alimony is money paid to support the wife (a few states now allow an award of alimony to a husband in an appropriate case). Once the parties come to an agreement as to the amount, they will find that the courts are reluctant to fix a different amount unless the sum agreed on is completely unreasonable.

True alimony, as distinguished from a lump-sum payment, relieves the husband of income tax liability on the payments to the wife, and makes the wife liable to pay income tax on the alimony she receives. How to distinguish what is alimony and what is not for tax purposes is explained in Chapter XII.

The time, place, and manner of payment of alimony and support should be set forth with precision—i.e., weekly, monthly, by mail to an address, by delivery to a lawyer's office, by money order, by check.

Escalation

Many separation agreements look ahead to the time when the husband (or wife) may be earning considerably more than is earned at the time of the agreement. Possibly, the next generation of contracts will take into account the effects of inflation and increase in the cost of living. Few present contracts contain such a provision. Courts are reluctant to grant increases on the sole grounds of inflation and cost-of-living change because they would be deluged with applications to modify their judgments.

Provision is often made that if the spouse's income shall increase beyond a certain fixed sum, then he or she shall increase the alimony and/or child support payments by a percentage of the increase. The parties can fix any percentage they please; but experience shows that when the percentage reaches about 40 percent and the husband's taxable income is about $30,000 per year, the husband begins to lose interest in earning more because he keeps so little of the excess.

Remarriage

Unless the agreement provides that alimony continue, it stops upon her remarriage (or the death of either spouse). It seems repugnant for the first husband to support another man's wife. However, there is no bar to an agreement to pay her a sum of money as long as she lives. In such case, if the agreement does not say specifically that her remarriage ends the alimony payments, they continue for her lifetime (See Chapter IX).

In New York State, by statute, a divorced wife who lives with another man and holds herself out to be his wife risks forfeiture of her alimony in a judgment of divorce but not her contract rights to support if the contract survived the judgment. The law is strictly interpreted; she does not forfeit alimony if she lives with another woman in a lesbian relationship. (It seems curious that although the New York courts recognize lesbian conduct as grounds for divorce, they do not consider it a ground for forfeiture of alimony.)

Fringe Benefits

Sensible parties try to protect their children's future. This is the primary reason a provision that the principal income producer, or both parties, undertake to maintain life insurance in an appropriate sum. The provision is meaningless unless it requires that the other spouse and/or the children be made irrevocable beneficiaries; that the insured not be allowed to borrow against the policy; and that in the event of failure to pay premiums, the other spouse be given notice and the opportunity to pay the premiums. If the irrevocable policy is delivered to the wife, the husband's payment of the premiums may be considered as alimony, not taxable to him and taxable to the wife.

Sometimes in order to give a divorced wife a better estimate of how much she will have available to live on, the husband may offer to pay income tax on the alimony. New York does not allow the husband to pay the wife's state income tax. The federal government has no such restriction. However, a simple agreement to pay the federal income tax has a hidden complication. Suppose alimony is fixed at $10,000 and the recipient must pay $2,000 tax. If he(she) receives an additional $2,000, that increases the alimony to $12,000, which in turn, requires additional income tax. The solution is to set aside a lump sum for the approximate tax and consider the lump sum as additional alimony.

In addition to other benefits, the parties may wish to provide for continued support in their wills. Normally, alimony and support cease upon the death of either party. But, by provision in a will it would be possible to create an estate (deceased person) obligation for continued payment of support until the recipient's death.

In the area of medical insurance, the parties generally provide that their medical insurance shall continue to cover their children; and they often provide that it shall continue to cover the divorced spouse. Medical insurance with such coverage is often free to employees and costs the party nothing. In the event of catastrophic illness, an unprotected divorced spouse may suffer economic disaster. Decency would demand that coverage be continued, especially when it is free.

Income Tax Information

The importance of considering the tax implication of a separation agreement cannot be overemphasized. Often this is the first point on which the parties can agree; and it leads to agreement on other points when the parties begin to understand that agreement is to their mutual advantage.

To safeguard that part of the agreement which concerns income tax, the parties should agree to have free access to each other's income tax returns wherever appropriate. For example, if the separation agreement is in contemplation of a divorce, the parties have the right to file a joint tax return if they are still married on December 31st of the taxable year. If the parties sign jointly, either one may be liable for any tax deficiency, fraud, or misrepresentation penalty due to the act of the other. Suppose the wife agreed to sign a joint return on the husband's assurance that he will pay the tax. The following year she is told that the husband has not paid, and, because she has signed jointly, she is equally liable for the tax payment. Her agreement should have provided for proof that the husband had paid. (See form of agreement on pages 153-155.)

Whenever there is an escalation clause which provides that if earnings change substantially for either party, the amount of alimony or child support may be increased or decreased accordingly, what better way to check the increase or decrease than to have the party's last tax return?

Counsel Fees

Counsel fees are based primarily on what the lawyer charges per hour. This in turn depends on his expertise, his overhead, his past experience with matrimonial actions. As with medical practice, a further consideration is the wealth of the client. A law firm that has an annual retainer from a client whose business practice gives the firm large fees might charge nothing for drawing a separation agreement or a will.

If either party has substantial income, it is wise to engage a lawyer who specializes in matrimonial matters. There is an American Academy of Matrimonial Lawyers which has diplomates in the same sense that the medical societies have diplomates for their specialties. Local bar associations can also be called for advice on choosing a lawyer. However, there are no official fee schedules; and a little shopping may well be in order. Good advice from a specialist is always worth the cost.

IX. What the Wife Should Look for in a Separation Agreement

Who among us has foresight enough to plan what to do with his earnings ten or twenty years in the future—or even next year? The best we can do is take advantage of the experience of lawyers and accountants skilled in the field of matrimonial agreements.

The following is a catalog of suggestions gleaned from extensive experience in drawing and examining marital agreements. It is a kind of universal catalog that should be altered to fit the individual.

SUPPORT FOR CHILDREN

Children's welfare is the paramount interest in the eyes of the court; and the court will not be bound by any agreement that is not considered to be in their best interests.

Provision must be made for their present needs: food, shelter, clothing, medical expenses, education, vacations, summer camps, amusement. If the father is to pay for part or all of these expenses, he should have a voice in choosing schools, in how money should be spent for vacations, music and dance lessons, etc.

The agreement should look to the future. Efforts should be made to set up a trust fund for college education; money should be allocated for special medical treatment if a child has an expensive chronic illness. A wife should make sure that she or her attorney is provided with hard evidence that the fund has been set up. An unenforced, or unenforceable provision is worthless.

Although the court is not bound by the provisions for child support, it will usually accept a reasonable agreement and refuse to modify it unless shown a substantial change of circumstances.

ALIMONY

More and more, as the public accepts equal rights for women, the courts tend to award less and less for alimony on the theory that the wife is capable of taking care of herself. A woman should be realistic in her alimony demands. In fixing alimony, a court considers these criteria: length of time of the marriage, age of the parties, earnings of the parties, earning capacity of the parties, number and age of children, who will have custody, marital standard of living before the break-up, and net worth of each of the parties.

Unless there are exceptional circumstances, the court will limit alimony to some figure between 20 and 40 percent of the husband's spendable income at the time of divorce, subject to the wife's potential earning capacity or income, and to the needs of the children.

Escalation of Alimony

The agreement may provide for escalation or reduction of alimony depending on the future earnings of the husband or wife. This is usually, but not necessarily, expressed as a percentage of future income. For example, "If, after the first year of this agreement, the husband's taxable income should be in excess of x, then he shall pay to the wife as additional alimony, 10% of the excess of such taxable income." The husband should be required to furnish a copy of his annual tax return as proof of his income.

Keep in mind that a former wife has no right to her ex-husband's good fortune. On the other hand, a wife who supports her husband while he is studying to become a lawyer or a doctor has created a potential for greater earnings which she should share. In a recent Florida case, the court ordered the husband, who had become a successful lawyer, to support his ex-wife and pay for her tuition while she attended medical school. She had supported him by working as a nurse while he studied to become a lawyer. A New York case, which involved an unusual award, allowed alimony well beyond the pre-divorce standard of living when it was shown that the husband had kept the household at a poverty level, plowing most of his earnings back into his business. Needless to say, the business became a great success immediately after the divorce and his income rose accordingly.

SURVIVAL OF THE AGREEMENT AFTER DIVORCE

Be aware that living apart following an agreement for a period of time is a ground for divorce in many states. (See the table at the end of Chapter III.) Some states do not allow an action for separation as distinguished from divorce, if the parties have already separated by agreement. Nor will the courts enforce an agreement that specifically buys a divorce (see p. 93).

There are three possible ways a future divorce judgment can deal with a separation agreement:

> 1. The judgment may provide that the agreement is "merged" (extinguished) and shall not survive the divorce. This does not prevent the divorce judgment from adopting many or all of the terms of the agreement.
>
> 2. The judgment may provide that the agreement is incorporated into the divorce judgment, but shall survive—i.e., the parties have a divorce judgment *and* a contract.

3. The divorce judgment may provide that the agreement is not incorporated, but shall survive—i.e., the parties have a divorce judgment and a contract, but the terms of one are not necessarily the terms of the other.*

What are the effects of the three different methods of treating separation agreements in divorce judgments?

If the separation agreement is extinguished, as in #1, the parties lose their right to treat the agreement as a contract. This is a valuable right because under the Fourteenth Amendment of the U.S. Constitution, no court has the right to change a valid agreement. But the judgment of a court is not so sacred. A court's divorce judgment may be changed by a later court for many reasons. There is no finality. In matrimonial actions, the original alimony and child support can often be modified at a later time by the court because of a substantial change in the circumstances of the parties or the needs of the child.

If, as in #2, the agreement is incorporated into the judgment, but the agreement survives, a wife has two remedies if her former husband defaults. She can sue on the agreement as a contract, obtain a money judgment for alimony and child support, and have the sheriff seize

*The appellate division of one section of the New York State Supreme Court has ruled that no divorce judgment may be submitted that seeks to incorporate a separation agreement. The terms of the agreement may be spelled out in the proposed judgment; but the court will not allow the whole agreement to be incorporated by reference. This saves the court from rubber-stamping agreements that may have unenforceable or inequitable terms.

enough of the husband's assets to pay the judgment. However, she can also apply to the equity part of the court to hold her husband in contempt of court for failing to follow the court's direction to pay alimony and child support. The penalty for contempt of court is fine and imprisonment until the order of the court is obeyed.

There is a drawback to #2. Should there be a change of circumstances sufficient for a court to grant an increase in alimony, the court will generally consider itself bound by the contract and will refuse to modify the judgment; this however is not true of child support. Husbands often prefer alternative #2 because they feel they have an assurance that their liability for alimony is fixed permanently—i.e., they know where they stand.

The third alternative invites lawsuits. The agreement cannot be changed even if the divorce judgment is changed at some later time—so the contract idea may work as a two-edged sword. In an extreme case, in which circumstances have changed so that payment of the agreement alimony and child support have become an intolerable burden for the husband, he can petition for relief from the court. The court may modify its judgment of alimony and child support downward and threaten to hold the wife in contempt if she sues on the contract. It is questionable whether a finding of contempt would be sustained on appeal. But the wife may not be interested in buying a second lawsuit on top of the first one.

On the other hand, should a wife's circumstances change substantially so that she might need an increase in alimony and/or child support, the court might modify the divorce judgment without regard to the agreement. The wife would then have the option of suing on the divorce judgment. If she were awarded an increase, she would have the option of suing on the divorce judgment to collect the increase under the threat that the husband might be held in contempt of court if he failed to pay.

In spite of the danger of getting involved in secondary lawsuits, alternative #3 might seem best for the wife. This is an area of the law that definitely requires the services of an expert. There are many "fine-print" clauses that can be added to an agreement to change or distort the effect of the possibilities of alternatives 1, 2, and 3 as outlined here.

Which alternative is best for the wife depends on the total picture. An attorney who specializes in matrimonial relations can give invaluable advice. He will make sure that there is a clear indication in the separation agreement to show what will happen to it in the event of a future divorce.

VISITATION

In most cases, a nonworking wife is given custody of very young children unless she is shown to be an unfit mother. When children are about age 10 and up, the courts begin to consider awarding custody of boys to the father and girls to the mother. When children are 15, the child's preference is given great weight. It is unwise to try to force an older child to live with a parent not of his/her choice. As mentioned in Chapter VIII, a face-saving device is to provide "joint custody," which is a meaningless term. What difference does it make if the mother is awarded custody but the child lives with the father most of the time? Naturally, some support arrangements would have to be made for the child's visitation with the mother. Generally, young children are not split up between the parents.

The agreement should contain an annual calendar showing clearly the time, place, and manner of visitation for the parent not having custody. This can be a touchy matter. Some years ago, a husband shot and killed his ex-wife in front of their horrified daughter who the wife had brought to a "neutral place" for visitation. If the parties cannot stand the sight of each other, it is best to arrange to have the child picked up at a church, or at the home of a mutual friend, or some other place where the parties need not see each other. If the parties are compatible, the child can be called for at the custodial parent's home. This is the more normal procedure.

Overnight stays will depend on the age and sex of the child. Obviously a 1-year-old will not ordinarily be subjected to an overnight stay with the noncustodial spouse.

Holy days and holidays should be alternated. Vacation time should be arranged in accordance with the parents' own vacation schedules.

It is very important to have a specific procedure for cancellations—the noncustodial parent should give several days' notice of a cancellation. No child should ever have to suffer because a parent suddenly fails to keep his/her appointment for visitation.

From the wife's point of view, it is better not to have support payments conditioned on granting visitation. If such a provision appears in the separation agreement, the husband is entitled to withhold support payments in the event he is denied visitation. If visitation depends solely on the terms of a divorce judgment, then the husband's remedy, if he is denied, is to apply to the court to punish his wife for contempt. As a practical matter, if the wife sues for child support that the husband has withheld, she will probably be compelled to allow visitation even though the judgment or the agreement does not make visitation a condition of payment.

In the battle between wives and husbands who insist on continuing their fight after they are divorced, the children are often used as potent weapons. This should not be allowed to occur—it can only hurt a child, and of course, does not help either parent.

It may be wise to consider limiting telephone calls to particular days of the week, and to a limited length of time.

Often, the wife will be asked not to permanently take the children outside the state, or outside a limited area. Logically the noncustodial parent's visitation rights would be nullified if the new residence were beyond a reasonable radius such as 75 miles. Exceptions can be carved out if the custodial parent remarries and the new spouse's residence is beyond this radius. Also, employment or health reasons as certified by a medical doctor might suffice. In such event the agreement should provide for extended visitation on holidays and during the summer recess.

THE MARITAL DWELLING

If the wife is to continue living in the house, apartment, cooperative, etc., there should be provision for her exclusive occupancy and for payment of the rent, mortgage, utilities, repairs, and whatever other expenses are necessary for maintenance. This should be spelled out clearly so that the ex-husband cannot say, at some later date, that a particular expense is not covered. The gardener's bill for an expensive Connecticut estate was $3,000 annually. That, said the husband, was not part of his agreement.

INSURANCE

Alimony and support stop with the death of the spouse who is obliged to pay. If there are children, a husband will often agree to maintain a life insurance policy for their benefit. Sometimes he will also make the wife a beneficiary on the theory that she will need money to support the children as well as herself when her alimony and child support payments cease. To protect the beneficiaries, the policy must make them "irrevocable beneficiaries." The wife should have written notice of unpaid premiums and the right to make payment if the husband defaults. If the policy is irrevocable and the wife is the beneficiary, the husband's payment of the premiums becomes alimony, tax deductible to him, and taxable to the wife as part of her alimony income. In such circumstances, it is best for the wife to have physical possession of the policy. Her designation as irrevocable beneficiary and record owner will also give her the rights to any cash surrender value in the policy.

Health insurance is very important. Many large companies give their employees and their families free health insurance. If possible, the agreement should continue the wife's coverage in addition to the children's coverage. If there is no such coverage, the husband should be required to maintain or procure adequate health insurance and proof that he has done so or agree to pay for any major medical expenses until the wife's remarriage.

COUNSEL FEES

The common-law rule is that a husband is liable for his wife's "necessaries"—i.e., reasonable food, shelter, clothing, and some services. Legal fees are considered to be "necessaries" and the husband is liable for them unless the wife has sufficient ability to pay her own fee, which may minimize the husband's responsibility to reimburse her for such payments. He should pay for a lawyer of the wife's choice, a lawyer who is of equal reputation and ability as his own. When the parties are not on bad terms with one another, they often try to save money by using one lawyer who is a friend to both. But a sensible lawyer will not agree to represent both parties, especially if he is a good friend of both. If he does, he may not be a good friend much longer.

TERMINATION OF ALIMONY AND SUPPORT

As mentioned in the section on insurance, the alimony awarded by the court ends with the death of either party. However, by a separation agreement, the spouse who has the duty to pay may bind his estate to continue to pay after his death. He may leave a lump sum, or a trust fund, or, as discussed earlier, an insurance policy.

New York State has a law that permits the ex-husband to stop alimony payments upon proof of the ex-wife's remarriage, or, in the court's discretion, to stop payment upon proof that the ex-wife is habitually living with another man and holding herself out as his wife. But a separation agreement may provide that alimony continue even though the ex-wife has remarried. There is no bar to such a contract provision in any of the states. The theory is that an ex-wife whose alimony is guaranteed after remarriage is a much better marriage prospect than one who will lose her alimony upon remarriage.

Support for children usually ends when they reach the age of 21. A definite age should be fixed for the cutoff of support, because with the trend toward reducing the age requirement for voting and responsibility to 18, the phrase "come of age" is ambiguous. There is no magic in the number "21." A separation agreement may provide for support for a child until he or she marries, enters military service, finishes college or graduate school, or becomes self-supporting. Sometimes a cutoff age of 22 is utilized, or whichever of the conditions should first occur.

EXCHANGE OF INFORMATION

Because the parties will live apart without moles-
tation from one another, there should be some procedure for the exchange of important information. Where
children are concerned, the agreement should provide
for notification if a child contracts a serious illness. The
party who pays for the treatment is entitled to a voice
in choosing the doctor, the hospital, and even the course
of treatment (for example, is an operation necessary?).
Notice that a child is too ill for visitation is a common
ploy to deprive a party of visitation rights, and the
courts are well aware of this device.

There should be conferences on choice of schools,
on religious instruction, on vacation plans, etc. These
decisions may be made informally; but if the parties
cannot deal calmly with one another, they should agree
to meet with their lawyers, or perhaps to submit such
disputes to arbitration.

These are some of the more important provisions
which, from the wife's point of view, should appear in
the separation agreement. The points discussed by no
means exhaust the subject, however.

X. What the Husband Should Look for in a Separation Agreement

There is very little difference in what the husband should look for and what the wife should look for in a separation agreement. The fundamentals are the same: a provision to live separate and apart, and clear terms for doing so. The conflict usually comes in determining how to pay for alimony and support.

SUPPORT FOR CHILDREN

We must assume that a father has the interests of his children at heart, and that he will provide for them to the best of his ability. How much cash this requires makes each case unique. There are two general guides:

the children's *needs,* which can be determined fairly accurately from a budget for the previous year; and the father's *means.* Although an ex-wife can seldom expect any increase in alimony due to her ex-husband's later good fortune, his children can expect increased support. Their allowance depends to a great extent upon his means.

In the event of the husband's remarriage, when the expense of a second family will make demands on his means, the courts consider that his primary obligation is to the first family.

Support payments for children are not deductible from the father's income for tax purposes. However, if the agreement specifies that the payments are made as alimony, not child support, then the payments are income to the mother and taxable to her. And the father can deduct these payments from his income. If the mother is in a tax bracket substantially lower than the father's, and if she has custody of the children, it will cost the husband no more to pay her a larger sum for alimony than it would cost him to pay a smaller sum for support. Thus, he can make more money available to the children at the expense of the Internal Revenue Service. The advantages of allocating a larger sum for alimony with the understanding that it is to be used for child support is discussed fully in Chapter XI.

ALIMONY

Call it "male chauvinism" or "machismo," few men expect alimony even in those states that allow an award of alimony to the husband. There are situations in which wealthy women have agreed to pay their husband for a divorce; but these are usually clandestine agreements that are probably unenforceable in the courts.

Escalation of Alimony

Agreements to pay a percentage of future increases in earnings are generally bad for the husband. Such agreements may be the result of guilt feelings at the time of the making of the agreement, or of revulsion; a man may feel he has transgressed and been caught, or he may be willing to give anything to escape from an unbearable marriage. The best course for the husband when he has such feelings is to let the agreement cool for a while and seek the advice of a matrimonial expert.

One young airline pilot earning $12,000 a year had become harassed to the point that he was willing to make any arrangement to secure a divorce. He felt his career was at stake, and life with his wife was unbearable. He signed a separation agreement that gave his wife 40 percent of any increase in his future earnings. Ten years later as a full-fledged airline pilot, his earnings were over $40,000 annually, plus fringe benefits. Considering his tax bracket, and the expenses of the second family which he had started several years after his divorce, there was little incentive for him to accept higher-salaried work with increased responsibilities. If he were to earn an additional $5,000, his ex-wife would receive $2,000 of it and he would have left only $3,000, more than half of which would go to federal, state, and city income taxes. He would end up with less than she did.

SURVIVAL OF THE AGREEMENT AFTER DIVORCE

The three possible ways a future divorce judgment can deal with a separation agreement are given on page 94 of Chapter VIII.

One aim of a separation agreement is to fix, as permanently as possible, the liability of the husband for alimony. It is clear that all courts hold that children are not bound by the agreement between their parents in regard to support, visitation, and custody. Unlike the adults, who are assumed to be fully responsible for their decisions, the court considers itself as a quasi-parent to the child and has the power to review these areas on proper application by either parent. Their financial needs may be fixed temporarily by an allowance that is reasonable at the time of signing the agreement; but if at a later time there is a substantial change of circumstances, the court may review its judgment and may raise or lower child support accordingly. But, remember, the court can modify only the judgment; it cannot alter the agreement when it survives the judgment. If the court, at a later time, reduces child support in the judgment, the wife may still bring a contract action for the amount of support called for in the agreement. Even bankruptcy does not relieve a husband from the obligations of an agreement to support an ex-spouse and children if it was made in good faith.

Which of the three possible methods of relating the separation agreement to the judgment of divorce is best for the husband?

1. (Agreement is merged and does not survive the divorce): In this case the terms of the agreement that are incorporated into the judgment hold until such time as there is a substantial change of circumstances. There is no finality, no guarantee that the ex-wife cannot successfully apply for an increase in alimony and/or child support at some future time. Neither is the husband barred from applying for a reduction of alimony and child support if he has suffered substantial reverses. It is a gamble.

2. (Agreement is incorporated into the divorce judgment but survives any future divorce judgment): In this case the courts will generally refuse to change the provisions for alimony if the ex-wife seeks an increase at a later date. When there is a danger that the ex-wife may become a public charge, the courts have found ways to avoid the agreement. However, even though alternative #2 may seem preferable, husbands should remember that this is a fixed obligation; they will not be released from their obligation in the agreement even though they might be able to show a substantial reduction in income and be able to seek a reduction of alimony or child support in the judgment of the court.

3. (Agreement is not incorporated into the judgment, but survives anyway): This is a bad bargain for the husband. He is bound, in the civil courts, by the contract terms (as in #2 above), which the courts can-

not change. But the wife is not barred from applying to the court for an upward modification of the alimony provision in the divorce judgment. If she succeeds in increasing the alimony, the husband is subject to contempt of court if he fails to pay the increase. But if he successfully petitions the court to make a downward revision, he is still liable for the larger amount in the civil court under the terms of the contract, provided his ex-wife is willing to undertake a second lawsuit.

VISITATION

It is to the husband's advantage to condition support payments upon visitation rights. Then, if the wife, who has custody, maliciously makes the children unavailable for visitation, the husband can withhold support. This is a poor weapon, though, because it is the children who suffer. There are other weapons, however. The separation agreement may provide that if the wife's conduct makes it necessary for the husband to bring a proceeding to obtain visitation, *and if he is successful,* the wife is liable for counsel fees and costs of the proceeding. These charges can be made deductible against her alimony, if any. But, again, the penalty hurts the children more than it hurts the wife. Even where violation is clear, courts are reluctant to put a woman into jail for contempt of court in a matrimonial situation.

The schedule for visitation should be made as explicit as possible so there can be no future argument about the details. Visitation should be planned for the benefit of the children, not for the benefit of the parents; and it is impossible to overemphasize the harm done to children who become pawns in their parents' war with one another.

Other thoughts on visitation may be found in Chapter VIII.

MARITAL DWELLING

In most cases, the wife continues to occupy the marital dwelling, especially if there are children in her custody and the husband moves out. There are exceptions, depending upon the circumstances.

In an agreement is is important to look ahead and provide for future living accommodations in the event of a divorce. If the parties occupy an apartment, the terms of the lease should be considered. Who gets the security, if any? Who is responsible on the lease? If the parties own a cooperative or a condominium, in whose name is title? Should the shares or title be sold? The same questions apply to real property.

If title to real property is in both parties' names, as husband and wife, they are considered tenants by the entirety. Each owns an undivided half of the property with a right of survivorship—if one dies, the other inherits the other half by law. As we have stated in earlier chapters, a tenancy by the entirety exists only as long as the parties remain married. The judgment of divorce ends that special kind of tenancy, and the parties become tenants in common. As tenants in common, each party owns one-half, and either party can start a proceeding to have the court arrange for the sale of the property and distribution of the proceeds.

INCOME TAXES

If an accountant is employed to prepare income tax statements, it is most sensible to have him work out comparative returns showing what the tax cost will be if money is paid to the wife as alimony or as child support. Further explanation and examples are given in Chapter XI.

It is vital for the husband to decide in advance what information he is willing to reveal in negotiations to fix alimony and support, and, if there is reason for it, what future information will be given. If the ex-husband is willing to agree to an escalation clause, it may be enough to agree to show only page 1 of future tax returns.

TERMINATION OF ALIMONY AND SUPPORT

Alimony ends automatically with the death of husband or wife. If a husband is in arrears in his alimony, the ex-wife may have a claim against his estate.

Alimony usually ends with the remarriage of the ex-wife; but it is possible to contract to pay her even after remarriage. However, if she does not remarry, and if she lives with another man, in a *de facto* husband and wife relationship, it is possible to stop alimony payments unless there is an agreement to pay even after remarriage. It may be difficult to prove such a *de facto* relationship, however. The courts recognize the change in morals and tend today not to penalize people for such arrangements.

Child support usually ends with marriage of the child, his/her entry into the armed forces, or the "coming of age" or "emancipation" of the child. As mentioned in Chapter VIII, now that the age of majority is considered to be 18 in many states, it may be possible in those states to cut off support liability at 18. In any event, the father should decide on a definite age for the termination of child support. The contingencies (marriage, graduation from college or graduate school) should be made definite, keeping in mind the circumstances that are appropriate.

EXCHANGE OF INFORMATION

Seldom do husband and wife part on really friendly terms. Most often, it remains an abrasive relationship, and time does not always heal the wounds.

Although the parties have separated, their agreement may call for contacts with each other with respect to their children, the division of property, the payment of alimony and support, insurance, etc. If the husband and wife part as friends, there is no problem. If not, they should be isolated from each other as much as possible. Information should be exchanged through their respective lawyers. Communications should be in writing. When documents are delivered, receipts should be obtained; when payments are made, they should be by check or money order, not cash. Confrontations should be avoided if possible.

This chapter and the preceding one have covered only highlights of the subject of what people should expect from separation agreements. The guidelines relate to the matters that most often appear when the parties come to their lawyers to draw up such an agreement. The explanations given here should enable the reader to have a better understanding of the discussion if ever he or she attends such a conference.

XI. Enforcement

Unless they have learned from bitter experience, very few laymen are aware of the difference between winning a lawsuit and winning the battle on which the suit is based. A few examples will point out the difference.

Some years ago, a woman sued the late Congressman Adam Clayton Powell for libel. She won the lawsuit and was granted very substantial damages. Then came the battle to collect. Powell ended his days outside the reach of the U.S. courts. He fought collection so bitterly that the cost of trying to collect rose astronomically, wiping out most of the money available for the judgment. This was a classic example of the problem of trying to collect against a resourceful debtor who will not pay.

Recently, there was a custody matter in the New

York State Supreme Court. There were three children involved—two boys, aged 4 and 7, and an 18-month-old girl. Their mother was French and a stranger in this country. Their wealthy father had brought the family to New York, ostensibly for a short visit, and they stayed at his New York City apartment. Almost at once, he sued for divorce and took himself off to Connecticut, where he had another home. Now he wanted visitation— the right to take the children to Connecticut on weekends instead of seeing them in the lobby of their apartment house.

"What does he do with an 18-month-old baby girl?" asked the mother. "The doorman thinks he is crazy. What will he do with the children in Connecticut? They are too young."

Taking the children out of the state did not seem unreasonable to the judge. But he was cautious. He made the father post a $25,000 bond for their return.

The bond was posted. Next weekend, the father took the children and left the state—for Paris! Whether the mother was able to collect enough on the bond to enable her to return to France, find the children, and bring an action there for their return is not known. By that time, the father had probably skipped to Switzerland.

In short, the order or judgment of the court is only a piece of paper. To make that piece of paper effective may be another matter altogether.

Obligations can be enforced only where there are responsible people, tied to employment or property within the area the court controls. Collection of the court's award of money is impossible if there is no money. To put some one in jail for wilfully refusing to pay, or to make the children available for custody or visitation, depends on catching the guilty party within the state that has ordered the jailing. Even though proceedings under the Uniform Support of Dependents Law, which has been adopted by most states and the Canadian provinces, provide for reciprocity,* the problem of finding and apprehending the person still remains.

With these cautions in mind, we can discuss the remedies available to the party who won the contest and now wants to collect the prize—i.e., alimony, support for children, visitation, or custody. A few states provide all of the following remedies; all states provide some of them.

ARREST

If before, during, or after trial the plaintiff can show that the defendant is a nonresident and there is danger that he or she is about to leave the state so that the court's direction will be ineffective, the court may order the defendant to be arrested. The usual situation involves a defendant, mother or father, who is a foreign citizen. The plaintiff produces information that the defendant has passports and has bought airline tickets to

---

*Reciprocity provides that the record of the proceedings in one state court can be sent outside that court's geographical area for an enforcement proceeding in the place where the guilty party is found.

---

leave the country. It is possible to obtain a court order directing the sheriff to arrest the defendant and bring that person before the court for a hearing. The court may discharge the defendant if it finds no need to hold him (i.e., if he/she provides security—posts a bond, surrenders passports, or gives other satisfactory assurances that he/she will not flee the jurisdiction of the court). This remedy is rarely used, however.

CONTEMPT

Once the court has given a direction to a party to perform an act (to pay money, to allow visitation, etc.), willful failure to perform that act may be considered contempt of court. The punishment for contempt of court is fine or imprisonment, or both. Usually, there is a two-step procedure. First the court finds that the person is in contempt for wilful failure to perform the act. Then, if the act is payment of a sum of money, the court directs that the party may "purge" (remove) the contempt by payment of a fine by a fixed date. Second, if the fine is not paid by the fixed date, application may be made to the court to jail the party— or the party may be jailed without further application to the court.

Contempt is considered a drastic remedy and the courts are reluctant to grant it if there is some other means to force compliance. Where failure to pay money is the contempt, the result is imprisonment for debt, a practice that has long been in disrepute. On the other hand, it is remarkable how many husbands who claim to have no assets and no income are able to find money to pay a judgment when they are faced with jail. This is a situation in which a judge must call on his experience, his intuition, and his good sense to help him make a right decision.

JUDGMENT

The award of alimony and support for children creates a debt on the part of the party obligated to pay. It is as much an obligation as if that party had contracted to pay. If there is a breach of the obligation by the payor, the payee may ask the court for leave to enter judgment for the amount of the arrears. If judgment is granted, and it is seldom refused, the holder of the judgment has all the usual remedies: he, or she, may file the judgment with the clerk of any county in the state in which the debtor has real property, and the judgment becomes a lien on the property. The judgment may be given to the sheriff with instructions to take any real or personal property of the judgment debtor, auction it off, and turn over so much of the proceeds received from the auction as will satisfy the judgment. Practically, this means that the holder of the judgment must find assets—real estate, a bank account, a stock market account, an automobile, an art collection—and tell the sheriff where to go to collect. The sheriff, with the authorization given him by the judgment, notifies the bank to pay to him, or he seizes the asset and, after taking his fees for his services, turns over the amount of the balance that satisfies the judgment.

A judgment obtained in a sister state will be honored under the Fourteenth Amendment of the Constitution and given full faith and credit. A judgment from a foreign government that demands payment of money will normally be honored in our state courts under the rule of comity.

SECURITY

Security has been mentioned before under the remedy of arrest. The court has discretion to release an arrested party who provides such security (bond posted, passport surrendered, etc.).

Suppose the woman who is snatched from the airport explains that she has return tickets, and her only purpose in traveling to the foreign country is to give her dying mother a last chance to see her grandchildren. Under these circumstances, a sympathetic judge might well allow the party to leave with the children, providing she filed a bond in an amount sufficient to insure her return.

Suppose a husband, out of sheer meanness, holds back alimony payments so that his ex-wife is compelled to bring one enforcement action after another to collect the support that the court has imposed. Under these circumstances, the court might require the husband to post a bond to be used the next time he fails to pay.

SEQUESTRATION

Sequestration is a legal name for using property instead of cash or a bond for security. Very often, the parties owned their own home as tenants by the entirety, or, after divorce, as tenants in common, or the family car or boat is in the name of the party obligated to pay, or that party owns a business or real estate which brings in an income. The court may appoint a receiver to seize the property, or the party's interest in the property. The receiver takes over the property, or the part of the property owned by the debtor, and proceeds to pay over the income as the court directs. If there is no income, the court's receiver may sell the property and deduct the amount of arrears from the defaulting spouse's share to pay the debt or to insure future payments.

STAY

A stay is like an injunction in that it forbids the party from taking certain action. In a matrimonial proceeding the stay is used to prevent the party in default from taking any affirmative action in the case. For example, that person can be stayed from asking that alimony be reduced; or from asking that certain property be turned over to him/her—there is no way a person can be stayed from defending the suit for divorce. Thus, the person must be allowed to prove that he/she is not guilty of the conduct on which the divorce suit is based. For example, in the case of a charge of adultery, the person cannot be prevented from offering proof at the trial that he or she is not guilty of this conduct. Furthermore, in states in which proof of adultery on the part of the plaintiff will defeat the action even if defendant is guilty of such conduct, the defendant will not be stayed from offering such proof as a defense.

WAGE DEDUCTIONS

This is one of the most effective methods of securing enforcement of an order to pay alimony and support. Garnishment is the general name for this type of collection, and it is most commonly used to collect on installment contracts where poor people who are judgment-proof have steady employment. With the leave of the court, a notice is served on the employer that he must deduct from his employee's salary, the amount fixed by the court. This money, taken from each paycheck, is forwarded to the party entitled to the money.

The percentage of salary that may be garnished is strictly limited by federal and state law. But a type of garnishment called matrimonial wage deduction orders are an exception. Because of the importance of the duty to support wives and children (and because they may become welfare cases if not supported) some courts place no limit on the percentage that may be taken. But the judge who fixes the percentage always tries to strike a balance so that he will not "kill the goose that lays the golden egg." Also, matrimonial wage deductions take precedence over other wage garnishments or assignments unless there is a specific law providing otherwise.

UNIFORM RECIPROCAL ENFORCEMENT OF SUPPORT ACT AND UNIFORM SUPPORT OF DEPENDENTS LAW

Flight has always been a favorite refuge for husbands and fathers who wish to avoid their obligation to provide for their wives and children. This is not the place to tell horror stories about deserted wives and abandoned children. They are so common that they have lost their impact. The situation, although somewhat better than it used to be, is still serious in spite of adoption by most of the states and the Canadian provinces of a uniform law to allow the deserted wife to sue in the state in which she lives, and to seek enforcement in the state to which her husband has fled. The purpose of this law is to secure support in civil proceedings for dependent wives and children from the persons legally responsible for their support, and to follow those persons wherever they may have settled.

The law applies to

1. The husband liable for support of his wife
2. The father liable for support of his child or children under 21 years of age
3. The mother liable for support of her child or children under 21 years of age whenever

the father is dead or cannot be found, or is incapable of supporting such child or children

4. The wife liable for support of her husband if he is incapable of supporting himself and is likely to become a public charge

Whenever the state or a public agency gives support to such a dependent person, it may use this code to enforce payment by the party responsible. As a practical matter, the party seeking enforcement goes to the matrimonial or family court of the state in which he or she resides and applies for alimony and support. The court takes testimony, and if it finds the claim justified, fixes alimony and support on a temporary basis. The papers are then forwarded to the state in which the other party resides. There, usually through the probation department of the second state, an attempt is made to find the misssing party and serve the papers. If he (or she) can be found, he is given the chance to defend, and his testimony is taken and forwarded to the first state. On the basis of all the testimony, the court of the first state makes its decision granting, or not granting, alimony and support. The decision is sent back to the second state, which then will enforce the decision to the best of its ability, sending back the money it collects.

Obviously, this is a complicated and tedious procedure. But it is better than nothing.

In an ideal world, enforcement would be unnecessary. Parents would provide adequately for their offspring; husbands and wives would agree on support, and would fulfill their obligations honestly—in fact, in an ideal world, perhaps divorce would not even be in existence. But this is not an ideal world, and despite the elaborate provisions for enforcement, support obligations become a football that is kicked back and forth between the parties until one or the other wins an advantage, or both parties tire and give up the struggle.

XII. Tax Aspects of Divorce and Separation

TAXES AND DIVORCE

There is an old story about three quarreling partners.
The only thing on which two of them could agree was
how little they should pay the third.

In a sense, Uncle Sam is the third partner when a
quarreling couple divide their income. If the couple can
agree on nothing else, they can usually agree on a plan
for alimony and child support that requires the smallest
tax payment.

JOINT RETURNS

Until the parties are divorced, they may file a joint
return; and many couples have planned not to allow the

divorce judgment to become final until after December 31st so that they might have the benefit of filing a joint return for that particular year.

Take the Jeffersons. He produces all of the family income. Suppose they quarrel in February, split in April, and finish their divorce suit late in December.

While they are still married, they may, by agreement, file a joint return, which is to the advantage of both. However, Mrs. Jefferson would be wise to have a lawyer draw an agreement to protect her from liability for additional taxes, penalties, or even criminal prosecution if an Internal Revenue Service audit turns up something at a later time. If the agreement is made before April 15th, a joint return may still be filed for the preceding year. If the judgment of divorce is signed after the 1st of the next year, a joint return may be filed for the prior year. But the privilege of filing a joint return ends if the parties are no longer married at the end of the year.

April 3, 19____

Dear (Spouse):

The purpose of this letter is to induce you to execute joint federal, state, and city tax returns for the calendar year 19____.

When presented to you, these returns will have been prepared from information supplied to the accountants by me.

In consideration of your agreement to execute the joint returns, I hereby:

1. Represent and warrant to you that to the best of my knowledge I have heretofore paid all income taxes on all joint returns previously filed by you and me, that no interest or

penalties are due or owing thereon, and that no tax deficiency proceeding is pending or threatened thereon.

2. Agree to pay all taxes due in connection with such joint returns when executed, and agree to indemnify you and hold you harmless from all taxes due thereon. Should there be additional tax assessments, penalties, interest, or additional payment of any kind to be made on account of such returns, I agree to pay and discharge the same (except to the extent that they are levied on account of income which you have failed to disclose), and agree to hold you free and harmless from and indemnified against any such charges and any expense or liability connected to such returns or in review or audit thereof.

3. Agree to furnish to your attorneys copies of all communications, notices, reports received by me or on my behalf with respect to such joint returns.

4. Agree to provide true and correct copies of executed joint tax returns to you simultaneously with their execution, and by signing this agreement neither you nor your counsel are deprived in any respect from your right to introduce evidence (whether or not it contradicts such joint returns) concerning the assets, income, expenses, and deductions available to me, in event it is deemed in your interest to introduce such evidence in any pending or future action or proceeding between us.

For your part, you agree that:

1. I shall have complete right to defend against and contest any proposed or actual assessment and to conduct all negotiations and audits through attorneys and accountants of my own selection and at my expense exclusively.

2. You will execute all amended returns and other documents reasonably required and otherwise give your cooperation in all respects in connection with the matter.

3. You will authorize your attorney to sign your name to any refund checks, it being understood that all refunds arising out of said joint returns shall belong to me.

It is understood that these terms and conditions are not to

be deemed modified or waived unless such modification or waiver is in writing and signed by both of us.

For my part I agree to all of the covenants set forth above which are undertakings on my part.

Cordially,

_____

Husband

Agreed to: (date)   Wife

There is an element of danger in filing a joint return when parties are on the verge of separation or divorce. What if one of the parties, consciously or unconsciously, prepares a return, signed jointly by the innocent spouse, which later results in a tax liability? If both signed, each is liable individually for the tax arrears. However, if the false statement omits more than 24 percent of the joint reported income and the other spouse establishes innocence, the Internal Revenue Service may decide it is not fair to penalize the innocent party.

The following extract from the Federal Tax Tables shows three categories of taxpayers and a sample of differences in taxes paid on certain amounts of taxable income.

Amount of Taxable Income	Joint Return Tax	% Tax on Excess	Head of House-hold Tax	% Tax on Excess	Individ-ual Tax	% Tax on Excess	Married Filing Separate Tax	% Tax on Excess
$12,000	$2,260	25%	$2,440	27%	$ 2,630	29%	$ 2,830	36%
$20,000	$4,380	32%	$4,800	35%	$ 5,230	38%	$ 6,070	48%
$32,000	$8,660	42%	$9,480	45%	$10,290	50%	$12,210	55%

The advantage of filing a joint return is obvious.

A joint return may be filed by a married couple so long as they are still married at the end of the year reported. If there are dependents (children), the party who maintains a household for them can usually file as "Head of Household." A single party files as an individual.

The tax reduction strategy is simple. The aim is for the parties, after the marriage is no longer viable, to arrive at the lowest possible figure for the sum of the taxes paid by both parties. Usually a joint return will provide the savings. Therefore, if both parties can show approximately the same taxable income by filing a joint return, they will pay less taxes. Uncle Sam gets less, and the parties have more money to divide between them.

There are other tax saving devices that can be used, such as those related to the payment of alimony. Suppose, in the short table set forth above, one party had taxable income of about $32,000 and the other party had nothing. After divorce, a joint return is not allowed. Therefore, as an individual, the party having the $32,000 income would pay either $10,290 plus 50% of the excess over $32,000 as an individual; as a "Household Head" he would pay $9,480 plus 45% on the excess. But, suppose the party earning $32,000 of taxable income pays out $12,000 as alimony for that year. Alimony is deductible to the payor. Taxable income is now only $20,000 for the payor and $12,000 for the spouse. If both file as individuals, the two together pay only a total of $7,860; and, if there is excess over the $20,000 and $12,000, the excess percentages are 38% and 29% instead of 42%. If one of the parties, as a result of their supervision and maintenance of a minor child, can file as head of household, the saving is even greater.

When either party has taxable income well over $32,000 a year, and there is alimony to be paid, it is well to keep in mind that Uncle Sam is paying a fair percentage of the bill. This is the result of the effect of the deductibility of alimony payments from the gross income earned by the spouse making the payments. The ability to deduct support, paid in the form of periodic alimony, reduces the taxable income and effectively creates a tax savings. Thus if a man were earning $32,000 per year and was divorced, assuming no deductions were available, his federal tax would be $10,290. If he paid his former wife $12,000 per year alimony, he could deduct these payments from his gross income and only pay $5,230 on a taxable income of $20,000 ($32,000 minus $12,000). In such situations, it is wise to consult a tax expert as well as a qualified matrimonial lawyer to find legitimate ways to minimize taxes.

WHO PAYS THE INCOME TAX ON ALIMONY?

Again, the basic rule is simple. The payor (some states provide that a wife may be required to pay alimony to a husband whose income is substantially lower than hers) deducts alimony from earned income. The receiver of the alimony is taxed as though the alimony were earned income.

WHO PAYS THE INCOME TAX
ON CHILD SUPPORT?

The rule is the opposite of the alimony rule. Neither the receiver of the child support payments nor the children pay tax on what is received. The payor cannot deduct child support payments from his earned income. This leads to some tricky situations, which are discussed later in the explanation of child support and the Lester case.

These simple, basic rules concerning alimony and child support become complicated when the parties make their own agreements, or the courts give directions in their judgments, to provide for child support and alimony. There are many unique, tailor-made arrangements that may result, and it is difficult to do more than give definitions and explain concepts which have become part of the law of marriage, divorce, child support, and taxation.

WHAT IS ALIMONY?

The Internal Revenue Service has shocked many a husband by demanding taxes on money he paid his wife, before or after divorce. The husband believed he was paying alimony deductible from his taxable income. The IRS says not all such payments are alimony.

How does the IRS define those payments which it calls "alimony" and which it allows the payor to deduct from his taxable income? The definition is arbitrary and comes from Section 71 of the Internal Revenue Code, and from the cases that have been decided in challenges to this section. It is an area that requires the expertise of an accountant, an attorney, or both.

Alimony has been defined as a periodic payment made by one spouse to the other pursuant to a judgment of divorce, separation, or annulment, or a written separation agreement. There must be a *written* agreement. In the case of an oral agreement the payments are considered a household allowance common to all family life.

"Periodic" is the key word in this context. It means payment for an indefinite time to end, for example, with the death of either party or the remarriage of the wife. The amount may vary (e.g., alimony to be 20 percent of earnings), but the indefinite time brings the duty to pay within the IRS definition of alimony.

There is another type of payment that is also considered alimony. It is a written agreement to pay a fixed sum of money in installments of no more than 10 percent per year. Thus, it will take at least ten or more years to pay the full amount.

Suppose a very rich man had agreed to pay one of his divorced wives $1,000,000 in a lump sum. He would not be allowed to deduct this payment from his taxable income if it were paid over a period of less than ten years. However, his attorneys would most certainly advise him to pay at the rate of $100,000 per year or less over a period of more than ten years. He would then be able to take credit for a deduction from taxable income for each of the ten or more years not to exceed 10 percent of the principal for each year.

There is another caution concerning lump-sum payments. If the money is squandered, and the recipient is in danger of becoming a public charge, the court in certain jurisdictions may order additional alimony payments at some later time.

CAPITAL GAINS TAXES AND PROPERTY SETTLEMENTS

In these inflationary times, the market value of some items might well be more than their original purchase prices. In a property settlement related to a divorce, if one party transfers ownership of any property to the other party, it is necessary to be aware of capital gains taxes, because these can be substantial in cases in which the parties have such things as valuable paintings, stamp collections, silver, real estate, etc. If the person who transfers ownership of such property is sole owner of that property, he or she alone is liable for any capital gains tax; however, if a couple owns property jointly, each is liable for one-half of that tax.

Suppose Archie Bunker finally comes to a parting of the ways with Edith, his long-suffering wife. With typical Archie Bunker generosity, he decides to give her, free and clear, all of their possessions for which he has no use—the sewing machine, the oversized refrigerator with the oversized beer compartment, the stereo, the car (if they had one), etc. Because Edith, as a housewife, has had no earnings during their marriage, all of these items, bought in Archie's name out of his earnings, might well be adjudged by a court to belong to him alone. Imagine his chagrin when he finds that he alone, then, will have to pay any capital gains tax due on these items.

Often, jointly owned property, or property held in the name of one spouse will be given to the other spouse as part of a court judgment or a separation agreement. This results in a transfer of title.

When there is a transfer of title, the IRS will look at the transaction to see if the fair market value of the property, when compared with the purchase price, will result in a profit. If there is a profit, it is taxable as a capital gain. The person who transfers the property pays the tax. The person receiving the property pays no tax. However, if there is no consideration for the transfer, there may be liability for a gift tax.

As a cautionary note, the reader must be warned that an agreement which openly declares that one spouse is paying the other to obtain a divorce is probably void in most states.

CHILD SUPPORT PAYMENTS

Unlike alimony, child support may not be deducted from earned income by the party who pays. However, unless child support is clearly distinguished from alimony payments, the IRS may consider all of a payment to be alimony.

Agreements, or directions in a judgment, which provide that a wife use the money received from the husband for support of herself and the children result in treatment of the entire sum as alimony upon which she must pay income tax. In *Commissioner* v. *Jerry Lester* 366 U.S. 299 (1961) referred to earlier in this section, the Supreme Court of the United States held that an implication that part of the money paid to the wife is to be used for support of the children is not enough to separate alimony payments from child support. Thus, a provision that a wife is to be paid $20,000 per year, to be reduced to $10,000 per year upon the death or coming of age of the couple's child (usually 21), makes that wife liable for income tax on the entire $20,000 and allows the husband to deduct that sum from his taxable income. To create an allocation between wife and child support, the agreement or judgment must state clearly that $10,000 is for support of the wife and $10,000 is child support. The federal courts have indicated that this is a harsh rule, and they have strained to overcome it in some recent cases. However, this technique can be a positive factor in marital settlements if used wisely in order to gain valuable income tax advantages as referred to previously.

DEDUCTION FOR DEPENDENT CHILD

The general rule is that the parent having custody of the dependent child for more than half the year may claim the $750 Federal Income Tax deduction for a dependent child. But there are exceptions.

The IRS will allow the deduction to the paying party who pays more than $600 per year per child for child support, provided the court judgment or the written agreement of the parties states that the paying party is to have the deduction.

Even if there is no agreement, a paying parent who provides more than $1,200 per year toward support of a child or children, may take the deduction(s) unless the custodial parent can show expenditures of more than $1,200. The parent who has the deduction may, in most cases, claim a deduction for medical and dental expenses incurred for the child.

There is another child-care deduction that is often overlooked. It applies whether the parents are divorced or happily living together. The provision, Internal Revenue Code, Section 214, is designed to help the working father or mother (or both) who has custody of him/her and is compelled to employ household help because there is no one to care for him/her while the parent(s) is working. The caretaker must not be a relative and the deduction is limited to $4,800 per year maximum.

The dependent child(ren) must be under the age of 15, or otherwise unable to care for himself; and the parent's adjusted gross income must be $35,000 or less in order to get the maximum benefit of $4,800. For every thousand dollars of adjusted gross income over $35,000, the allowance is reduced by $500. If the parent has a gross income of $44,600, the allowance is wiped out—i.e., the difference between $44,600 and $35,000 is $9,600. At the rate of $500 deducted for every thousand dollars over $35,000, the allowance is reduced by $4,800, leaving nothing.

If the custodial parent spends less than $400 per

month for necessary household help under this provision, only the money actually spent can be claimed.

FAMILY HOME PAYMENTS

Which parent may deduct such payments from taxable income depends on such factors as whether the home is owned jointly, whether it is in the name of only one of the parties, and whether payments are made on a mortgage.

If the husband owns the home and the court orders that the wife may live there rent-free indefinitely, in addition to receiving "periodic payments of alimony and support," the husband cannot deduct the rental value of the home from his taxable income. The IRS takes the position that the court has ordered a transfer of property. His payments are not considered the payment of alimony.

If the husband does not own the home, and is liable on the mortgage and makes mortgage payments, this is for the wife's benefit and he may take the deduction and she is taxed as though the payments were income to her.

In general, these are the main questions concerned in family home payments:

1. Do the payments result in a discharge of the wife's personal obligation on the mortgage?

2. Do the payments increase her ownership of the property?

Such payments result in current economic benefit to the wife, and she is required to treat the payments as taxable income.

Suppose the husband and wife own their home jointly. If the husband's payment of the mortgage installments confers a benefit on the wife, one-half of the payment is considered to be alimony deductible by the husband and taxable income to the wife.

LIFE INSURANCE PREMIUMS

Premiums paid on the husband's life insurance policy become alimony, deductible from his taxable income, only if the wife is the irrevocable beneficiary and the policy is absolutely assigned to her. If there is a provision that if the wife dies before the husband the policy reverts to him and he may designate a new beneficiary, then the insurance premiums are not alimony and the husband cannot deduct these premium payments from his taxable income.

COUNSEL FEES

Counsel fees paid by the wife to obtain the alimony awarded to her are fees paid to obtain taxable income. Therefore, they are deductible by her. Counsel fees paid by her to obtain custody of her children are not deductible. If one counsel fee is paid for both services, the IRS will accept a fair allocation.

Counsel fees paid by the husband for services rendered to his wife or ex-wife are not income to her and she pays no tax; nor can the husband deduct these fees from his taxable income. They are not alimony.

Counsel fees paid by the husband to his own attorney are deductible from his taxable income only to the extent that the services pertain to tax advice.

LUMP-SUM SETTLEMENTS

Often, after several years of paying alimony pursuant to a court judgment or a separation agreement, the parties will negotiate a lump-sum settlement. Sometimes the ex-wife wants the settlement because she plans to remarry. (Unless the agreement provides clearly that alimony is to continue after the wife's remarriage, it is presumed that alimony stops. In New York State, the Domestic Relations Law, Section 248, provides that if the ex-wife is habitually living with another man and holding herself out as his wife, the husband will be relieved of his obligation to pay alimony.)

Sometimes the ex-husband has made an agreement that becomes psychologically and financially burdensome. Suppose he wants to remarry, for example, and doesn't want to have to pay his ex-wife indefinitely. In this case he can sometimes make arrangements to pay a substantial lump sum to her to end his alimony obligation once and for all.

A lump-sum settlement is deductible from the payor's taxable income and is taxable to the spouse who receives it *only* if it qualifies as a periodic payment. Arrangements for a lump-sum settlement should be checked by a qualified matrimonial lawyer or a tax accountant, or both.

There is a device called an *alimony trust* which is often used to effectuate such a settlement. Setting up an alimony trust requires expert advice to fit the individuals' circumstances. When the payor is in the upper income tax brackets, he may find that such a settlement saves him substantial tax dollars. The payment comes off the top of his earnings, the portion that is taxable at the highest rate.

ARREARS

When the wife successfully collects arrears of alimony previously withheld by her husband, the money she receives becomes income taxable to her in the year in which she receives it, no matter how far back the date when the money was first withheld.

Matrimonial tax law is a difficult specialized field. Reason and logic often say "Yes" when the IRS says "No." It cannot be overemphasized that this is not a field for the neophyte. Parties who have matrimonial litigation are well-advised to engage counsel with a good knowledge of the tax law.

XIII. Retainer Agreements and Counsel Fees

One of the most vital areas for the client to evaluate at the beginning of the professional relationship is the fee arrangement. By establishing a clear understanding at the outset, the client and attorney can avoid the possibility of financial misunderstandings later on.

Because the attorney is being paid a fee for services to be rendered, it is necessary to establish what services will be performed on behalf of the client, how much these services will cost, when the representation is to be deemed concluded, and what the attorney's fee requirements are. Each of these areas has direct application to the client, the marital negotiation, and the future relationship of client and attorney. It is human nature to want to know the rules of a business relationship, especially when the life or death of a marriage is being placed in the hands of a third party. It should be professionally natural for the attorney to meet that need clearly and matter-of-factly.

The most effective method is to clarify the arrangement in a written retainer agreement, signed by both parties, in which applicable terms and provisions are spelled out. Yet this major area is often overlooked by the prospective client and many attorneys do not bother to clarify such details for the client. The adversary attitude that characterizes many "divorce lawyers" seems to affect their relationships with their own clients. Thus many prospective clients are never allowed to understand the economic implications of the services to be rendered. In the dark to begin with, they remain at the economic mercy of their own attorney.

Many lawyers offer their clients written letters of agreement, but these documents do not always tell a client about other factors that, if known initially, might change the client's view. Various kinds of agreements are available. The prospective client has an absolute right to request any one or combination of them and to study the terms in advance of signing.

RETAINER AGAINST TIME

In this arrangement, the client pays an initial retainer to the attorney for services to be rendered. The client is advised of the attorney's hourly office rate and possible disbursements that may arise in connection with the services agreed upon. Examples of these are long-distance telephone calls, duplicating charges, over-time stenographic services, investigation services, and general court fees, to name a few. The retainer acts as a security fund for both lawyer and client and is generally geared to the average period of time the attorney feels will be required to complete the work. Of course, this estimate must be flexible.

In this type of agreement the attorney clearly sets forth the nature of the services to be performed, and promises that if the time expended on behalf of the client is less than the retainer provides for, a refund of the difference will be made. If the client is a wife, she may be entitled to a refund of part or all of the retainer. This can occur when the conclusion of the matter generates a fee paid to her attorney by the husband, either through agreement or by virtue of a court order or judgment. This contingency must also be provided for in the reimbursement agreement.

A sample of the retainer letter will clarify the form and content described above.

Dear Ms. Halsey,

You have consulted me with respect to matrimonial difficulties. We have agreed that I will represent you with respect to these difficulties.

I have advised you that an advance retainer of $ _____ will be required. My billable hourly office rate is $ _____ . In the event that the time expended by me in your representation exceeds the amount of the retainer, you have agreed to pay any additional sums billed to you based upon such additional time. Disbursements will be billed separately.

In the event that your matter is concluded in less than the time represented by the retainer, then you will be entitled to a refund of any difference that exists, subject to disbursements.

Furthermore, in the event that I receive a fee from your husband as part of the current negotiations, or through a court order, I will refund that amount to you subject to being paid my fee, as above set forth, for my time.

If this agreement is in accord with our understanding, please execute the enclosed copy of this letter and return it to me as promptly as possible.

Cordially,

John Doe, Esq.

Agreed and consented to:

_____

Ms. Annette Halsey

SET FEE PLUS DISBURSEMENTS

Under this type of agreement, the attorney and client determine in advance the amount of the fee for services to be rendered. Disbursements are billed separately.

Certain practical and substantive difficulties exist in this type of fee arrangement for the client as well as for the attorney.

For the most part, it is impossible for the attorney to determine in advance the exact amount and nature of the work to be performed on behalf of the client. Except when a clear-cut procedure is established in advance by agreement between the spouses, the time factor can be altered by countless possibilities.

Too often the attorney will function as a programmed machine when the nature of the retention is on a straight fee basis, unless the fee is substantial. If it is substantial, will the attorney be motivated to try for a reconciliation? Too often the agreement between attorney and client will not specify reimbursement.

When one considers that it takes time to get used to another individual in any kind of relationship, whether social or business, it becomes clear that the client will need time to determine fully the attitude of his lawyer. The attorney too will need to explore his client's true needs. Thus it would be incongruous for an attorney to agree to a large, nonrefundable fee in advance unless money was no object to the client. In that case, each deserves the other.

STRAIGHT TIME

This type of agreement is similar to the retainer against time. It is fair provided the attorney's hourly rate is reasonable. Again, the concept of reimbursement should be stated in any such agreement with a wife if financial circumstances and local laws permit.

RETAINER PLUS BONUS

This type of fee arrangement seems to be in vogue today. It is generally used by that small segment of the profession who should *not* be consulted if one has a marital problem. It promotes war and destruction. The bonus is usually geared to either the amount a husband can save in payment of support and property distribution or the acquisition of this in reverse by the wife. Of course, the entire emphasis in the representation would be to plot out and effectuate a "victory." In the end, no sane victory would be won.

An example of this type of business arrangement occurred recently with a female client who was 64, lived in a modest house in New Jersey and had one emancipated daughter and a son who was to start college in a few months. She was suffering from a diabetic condition, minor heart trouble, and mild depression. After thirty-seven years of marriage, her husband had abandoned her and the boy. He ran off with a young woman, removed all their cash and other valuable property, and now was out of the state. He also stopped supporting her, refused to pay for necessary drugs for her various conditions, and threatened not to pay the boy's college tuition that would soon fall due.

The husband's attorney stated that he had little control over his client. Furthermore, he, on behalf of his client, was insisting on a sale of the jointly owned marital home and would be getting a part of his fee from the proceeds. He also said that the wife should look to the sale of the house if her attorney wanted a reasonable fee from the husband for services rendered on behalf of the wife. The sale of the house was, under the circumstances, unnecessary for a proper settlement since the husband had substantial cash and other assets.

For five months, futile attempts were made to settle the case without the sale of the house as a condition. More and more pressure was brought to bear on the wife. Her husband stopped paying for gas and electric service in the dead of winter. Finally, the wife committed suicide. The house went to the husband as a matter of law in the state in which the parties resided.

Though there are many types of arrangements that can be made between client and attorney as to fees, perhaps the most important criterion is fairness to both parties. This is best accomplished by clarity of understanding right at the inception of the representation. The skilled professional should not hesitate to provide this with or without being requested by the client.

XIV. Conciliation

The fairy tales lied when they said, ". . . and they lived happily ever after." No couple, married or not, can live together for an appreciable time without some disagreement. Disagreements range from the trivial to the catastrophic; and the purpose of conciliation proceedings is to draw a line between the hopeless and the hopeful, and to advise how a marriage can be saved.

All states pay lip service to the concept that every effort should be made to save a marriage before the parties start an action for divorce. Our social structure is based on the theory that people marry and have children who are raised within the structure of the family, and that those children continue the cycle by marrying and raising their children within the same structure. The structure has survived throughout recorded history. But there are other possible structures. The Nazis, for example, experimented with the idea of having supermen and superwomen brought together for breeding purposes. They were supposed to produce genetically superior children who would be brought up apart from their parents, under the supervision of the state. The parents were not allowed family life. This structure did not work; and German culture still embraces the ancient concept of the family.

When a marriage has turned sour, the state is faced with the choice of forcing the couple to live together or allowing them to live apart. We are now in a cycle in which the state is relaxing its effort to force a couple to live together, and is softening its attitude toward living apart. Conciliation might be considered as a brake to hold back the rush to divorce. But in recent years there has been less and less emphasis on conciliation; there is even a tendency to treat it perfunctorily.

When, in 1966, New York State reformed its divorce law to allow five grounds other than adultery, it provided for compulsory conciliation. No divorce would be granted without a certificate from a "Conciliation Commissioner" stating that there was no further need for conciliation. By 1973, two things had become obvious: the state was spending a lot of money for very little result; and the only practical effect of the law was to delay divorce actions for a few weeks. When the law was repealed, Haiti and the Dominican Republic suffered a loss in their quickie divorce business.

Two states, Maine and New Hampshire, still compel the parties to try for a reconciliation when the ground for divorce is "irreconcilable differences." Maine requires a copy of a report by a court-approved professional counselor indicating that attempted conciliation has been unsuccessful. New Hampshire gives the trial judge discretion to compel counseling if there is thought to be a reasonable possibility of reconciliation.

Nevertheless, like the presumption of innocence in a criminal trial, one should always presume that there is hope for conciliation unless there is proof beyond a reasonable doubt that conciliation will fail. One judge in a matrimonial court always opened the proceedings by calling the parties up to the bench and saying, "There was a time when you were in love with each other. Isn't there some chance that you can bring that time back?" He would then ask about marriage counseling—had they tried it? Had they been to a religious advisor? to an analyst? Sometimes the couple took the advice and it was effective. Sometimes it was hopeless.

The most sensible approach to conciliation and the settling of family disputes if court-sponsored conciliation fails is to apply to one of several organizations that have set up machinery for a humanistic, ethical procedure to help in these situations.

The parties are urged to appear before an impartial panel of experts—experts who are qualified in those areas in which there is friction between the parties. As may be necessary, the parties are interviewed by a psychiatrist, a psychologist, a sociologist, a marriage counselor, a medical doctor, a tax expert, a certified accountant, a financial manager, a career counselor, a religious leader, an educator, and/or any other appropriate expert. Each party may be represented by an attorney; but this is in no sense a legal proceeding. The lawyers are observers, not participants. The panelists may employ case workers to investigate the statements made by the parties. No one is put under oath; there is no cross-examination, nor are there rules of evidence.

The experts meet with the parties, discuss the matters presented to them, and each member of the panel makes a report. The preliminary question is always: "Can this couple continue to live together?" If the answer is "No," the panelists go on to the questions of property, support, custody of children, visitation, etc. The panel then has a second meeting at which they present their recommendations to the parties and justify them. The parties are free to accept the recommendations (e.g., for conciliation, therapy, temporary separation, divorce) or refuse them. Each party is given a written report containing the panel's suggested guide for their future conduct whether they are reconciled or divorced. If the decision is for divorce, the parties have an unbiased plan for custody, visitation, and disposition of their property which, if they follow it, will avoid a costly and often vicious court contest in which a busy judge, rather than a panel of experts, fixes the rules for their future relations. How much better to come to court with these matters already taken care of in a nonadversary proceeding.

In this book we have tried to present both a practical and a legal understanding of the laws and special areas of interest surrounding marriage and family disunity. Usually it is with a hardened negative mental attitude toward the marriage that the spouse enters the portals of the lawyer's office. Yet it is our hope that other avenues of approach can and will be utilized before such final decision is made. If divorce is inevitable, perhaps this book will provide a greater sense of understanding of both the legal and human complexities that most assuredly trail behind every broken marriage. If we have brought about some slight clarification in the mind of the public regarding this vital area of our social structure, then there will be more reason to believe that reasonable and rational conduct will be the mainstay in the ebbing dream of marital harmony.

Glossary

abandonment: Marital abandonment is the unjustified leaving by one spouse of the other with intent not to return, and without the consent of the other.

adultery: Voluntary intercourse of a sexual or deviate nature between a party to a marriage and someone other than his or her spouse. Deviate sexual conduct refers to homosexual relations, sodomy, etc.

agreement: In marital matters generally labeled "separation" agreement or "property" agreement. An agreement is a contract. A contract is a legal concept by which two parties mutually promise to give some particular thing, or to do or abstain from doing a particular act, in such fashion that their promises are enforceable by law. Examples: to pay alimony, to allow visitation.

alimony: "The high cost of leaving." The obligation of one divorced spouse to provide for the support of the other. Alimony should be distinguished from child support, which is treated differently for tax purposes and for modification by the court.

annulment: A declaration by a court that no marriage was created by the marriage ceremony. In contrast to divorce or dissolution, annulment goes back to the start of the marriage.

bigamy: The crime of marrying while one has a living spouse from whom one has not been validly divorced.

child support: The obligation of a parent to provide for offspring. The obligation is usually limited to children who are not emancipated (over 18 or 21, married, in military service, self-supporting).

cohabit: In marital matters this means living together as husband and wife in the sexual sense.

comity: The principle of having our courts give effect to the judgment of a foreign country. The Fourteenth Amendment to the U.S. Constitution requires that each state give full faith and credit to the judgment of every other state. There is no requirement that the judgments of foreign countries receive such treatment. However, our courts generally treat the judgment of a foreign country as though it were the judgment of a sister state—unless the nature of the foreign judgment is repugnant to our laws or public policy. Thus a Mexican, Dominican, or Haitian divorce is recognized in most states provided the laws of those countries are strictly observed.

common law: A system of law, rules, and precedents we have inherited from the English system, as modified by our own history, precedents, and practices. Common law is distinguished from "statutory law"—the laws passed by Congress and the state legislatures. Most laws concerning matrimonial matters are statutory. Common law is also distinguished from "civil law," which in this context means the law inherited from the Roman system. Those states that are in areas formerly controlled by Spain still have vestiges of civil law, such as "community property" (Florida, Louisiana, Texas, Arizona, New Mexico, California, Washington, Idaho and Puerto Rico).

community property: Property acquired by the husband and wife during their marriage.

contempt of court: A willful contravention of judicial mandate tending to impede or impair its orders or judgments.

contract (see *agreement*): Contract is a word of "art" in legal matters. It is not a simple concept; and law students usually find this a required course during their first year. A legal contract obliges each party to do certain things in return for the other party's obligation to do certain things. Examples: to pay alimony and support, to divide property of the parties, etc.

cruelty: Cruelty of a nature sufficient for a court to grant a divorce is an undefinable term. The general test, with many exceptions, is that it should be such conduct as is designed to result in a loss of physical or mental well-being on the part of the other partner to the marriage as makes further living together harmful. The acts or failures to act that will achieve such results are countless.

decision: Decision should be distinguished from judgment or order of the court, although they are often combined in one paper. Before a judge grants a divorce, custody, temporary alimony, or other relief, certain facts must be presented:

> 1. For divorce, for example, there must be proof of the marriage.
> 2. There must be proof to satisfy the residence requirements.
> 3. There must be proof of the grounds for divorce sufficient to satisfy the state's law.
> 4. There must be proof that the defendant has been given the required notice of the hearing—at least that he or she has been served with a summons in the action.
> 5. There must be proof of such other matters as the state's laws may require.

A decision (sometimes called *findings of fact*

and *conclusion of law*) is the trial judge's recital that he is satisfied that the necessary facts have been proved. He concludes from this that he will grant a judgment of divorce. The lawyer for the successful party then prepares a judgment for the judge to sign.

The parties are not divorced until the judgment is signed. If one of the parties should die between the time of the decision and the signing of the judgment, it is probable that the divorce is aborted. Inheritance would follow as though the parties were still married. Remarriage to another during the period after decision and before the signing of the judgment would probably result in a bigamous marriage (see *interlocutory judgment*).

de facto: Law Latin for "in fact." Thus a couple may be separated *de facto,* meaning they are living apart as though they had a court-ordered judgment of separation. Their living apart has no legal effect with respect to property, debts, etc., except that it might furnish ground for divorce after a required period of living apart.

de jure: Law Latin for "by law" as opposed to the *de facto* situation. The inheritance and tax situations may be affected differently if the parties are separated *de jure* as opposed to *de facto.*

dissolution: Another word for divorce as used in some states. In other states it indicates a court direction for the termination of a marriage for special reasons not within that state's grounds for divorce. For example, in New York State, unexplained absence of a spouse for more than five years coupled with a belief that the spouse is dead is cause for dissolution.

divorce: termination of the marriage relationship and the marriage contract by direction of a court.

domicile—residence: domicile is the place where a person makes his home. He may have several residences, but, theoretically, only one domicile. A few of the tests for domicile are:

1. The place where a person lives most of the year
2. The place where a person votes
3. The place where a person pays taxes

Other indications of domicile are bank, auto registration, clubs, etc.

Residence is often misused as a synonym for domicile. For example, New York State requires one or two years "residence" by a party to make him eligible to apply to the New York courts for a divorce. It is understood that "residence" in this case means domicile.

emancipation: The change in legal status of an infant, minor, or dependent child when he or she has become an adult. Formerly, the age was 21; it is now 18 in many states for many purposes—e.g., voting, business transactions, the right to marry without parental consent. Note: New York State emancipates children at 18; but in that state, a father is still liable for support for a child until he becomes 21.

equity: The word has several legal meanings. The equity courts administered a system of law developed in England and adopted in the United States to supplement the common law. Common law was dispensed in the traditional courts according to rigid rules of procedure. When the case did not fit the traditional pattern, the parties might appeal to the "King's Conscience" through his Chancellor, asking that the king do justice or "equity" between the parties. Thus, a court and a procedure grew up administered by the chancellor in the equity court.

Equity is still used as a synonym for justice; for example, parties ask for equitable relief. Matrimonial matters were not allowed in the common-law courts, and the parties were compelled to come to the chancellor's equity court.

Equity also means a share, as a shareholder's equity in a business.

fraud: Fraud, in connection with an action to annul a marriage, consists of several elements:

1. There must be a false statement, or concealment of a statement which the party has a duty to reveal.

2. The statement must be material (e.g., that the party had never married before; is free from venereal disease; although previously married, has never had children, etc.).

3. The party making the statement must know at the time that it is false, or by "reasonable" standards, must know there is a duty to reveal what is being concealed.

4. The other party would not have entered into the marriage if the true fact had been revealed.

garnishment: A statutory proceeding whereby personal property, money, or credits in possession or under control of, or owing by another are applied to payment of debtor's obligation to a third person by proper statutory process against debtor and garnishee.

incompetent: A person who is not legally responsible. An adult person must be declared incompetent by a court in order to avoid the legal consequences of his/her acts. To some extent, an infant may gain the benefit of his act and yet disclaim responsibility if it is to his/her advantage.

infant: A minor, a person not of legal age. For federal tax purposes, a dependent child under 21 years of age is considered an infant irrespective of state law. In many states, infancy ends at age 18.

interlocutory judgment of divorce: This is a provisional judgment that does not become final until some later event. Many states do not allow divorced parties to remarry for six or twelve months after the decision granting their divorce. If the judgment or decree issued by the court is "interlocutory," and if a party marries another during that period, the second marriage is void.

joint tenancy (see *tenancy, joint*)

judgment—decree (*order, ruling*): Judgment or decree is the name used for the final direction of a court declaring the rights of the parties. An "order" is the court's direction concerning an intermediate application for some relief granted by the court. Examples: an order for temporary alimony, an order awarding custody pending a final judgment.

A *ruling* is a narrower determination generally made during trial by the judge presiding. For example, when a lawyer objects to a question, the judge responds, "Objection over*ruled.*"

jurisdiction (compare with *venue*): Jurisdiction has several legal meanings:

> 1. One meaning has to do with geographical considerations—the territory over which a court has power. For example, the police and law enforcement officers of a state can act only within that state's territory; county officers can act only within the county. They have no jurisdiction outside their territorial limits. To enforce a judgment outside the state that issued it, a party must take the judgment to the state where the judgment debtor has property, or where he can be found. The second state must be asked to give "full faith and credit" to the judgment. The second state will

then order its law enforcement officers to act within its territory—i.e., within its jurisdiction.

2. Jurisdiction of the type of action is limited in certain courts. Thus a family court has no jurisdiction to try a murder case or a traffic violation. The traffic court has no jurisdiction to hear a divorce action. In each state there is a court of "original" jurisdiction which has the power to hear any kind of suit brought in the state; but, although it may have the power, for administrative reasons it will transfer the case to a different (generally a lower) court.

3. Jurisdiction of the person is from the Latin—*in personam jurisdiction.* In our system of law, a person's rights cannot be affected by a court unless there is "due process." One of the aspects of due process is that proper notice must be given the defendant in every lawsuit. What is due process and proper notice is subject to devious, tortuous, and obscure interpretation from the layman's point of view. Stated very broadly, proper notice is service of a summons on a person within the state. There are many exceptions. Once the court has jurisdiction over the person of the defendant, the court has the right to make judgments and orders concerning his personal liberty, personal and real property, the dissolution of his marriage, the custody of his children, and his obligation to pay alimony and support, etc.

4. In jurisdiction of property (*jurisdictio in rem*), the state has the power to make disposition of all of a person's property found within the state. This applies to both real estate and personal property.

5. There is, finally, jurisdiction of the marriage. The marriage status is considered to be with each spouse. Thus the marriage status can be in two places at the same time. If a husband and wife go to two different states and each starts an action for divorce that is proper and valid according to the laws of each state, the courts will generally honor the judgment of the court of the state in which the first action was begun. If a spouse satisfies the domicile requirements of the state (six weeks in several states) and if some kind of notice is given to the defending spouse (publication in an obscure local newspaper may be enough), a state may grant a divorce dissolving a marriage. Sister states will give full faith and credit to the dissolution of the marriage status—but they may refuse to give effect to the other directions in the divorce judgment (e.g., provisions for the payment of alimony, disposition of property, etc.). Unless the defending spouse is a resident of the state, or, if a nonresident, he has been served personally within the state, his property cannot be touched and the courts where he resides will refuse to enforce a personal judgment against him.

minor: One not of legal age. An "infant," one not yet "emancipated"—i.e., too young to marry without parental consent, to make binding business agreements. Still entitled to parental support.

order (see *judgment*)

order of protection: This a special type of order usually issued by a family court, prohibiting one spouse from interfering with the other. For example, where the wife complains of physical assaults, she may persuade the court to issue an order directing the husband to stay away from the marital home. Where the husband complains that the wife phones his employer or his place of business and vilifies him to his associates or customers, the court may issue an order to the wife prohibiting such conduct. Disobeying such an order is contempt of court, punishable by fine and imprisonment.

pendente lite (law Latin): "During litigation," as in an award of alimony *pendente lite*. This is temporary alimony paid the party for living expenses until the court can make an award of permanent alimony in the judgment that will be signed after the trial.

periodic payment: This is a tax term used in the Internal Revenue Code which defines alimony payments that are deductible from the payer's income. The payments must be support payments for a definite amount of money (it may increase or decrease or be a percentage of earnings). It must be payable over a period of not less than ten years at not more than 10 percent of the total in any one year, unless terminated sooner by the death of either party or the remarriage of the dependent party. The payments must be made pursuant to a written agreement or a court order.

personal property: Also called "personalty." Property that is not land and buildings. Examples: money, stocks, bonds, jewelry, books, paintings, automobiles, anything movable and not attached to the land or a building.

real property: Also called "realty." Land, buildings, real estate as opposed to personal property.

reciprocity: A term used in international law denoting the relationship existing between two states when each of them gives the citizens of the other certain privileges on condition that its own citizens enjoy similar privileges.

separation: A "legal" separation is a direction by the court that the parties live apart. The marriage continues; marital rights, other than the right to live together, are preserved unless changed by an agreement between the parties. Living together implies sexual relations. A legal separation does not deprive a wife of her right to inherit from her husband unless, by a separation agreement, she has agreed to give up those rights which the law allows her to give up.

sequestration: A procedure by which a husband's property is seized so that the wife may obtain payment of alimony or child support. The court, in a proper case, appoints a receiver of the property who takes over, collects the rents or income from a business, or sells the property upon instructions from the court. The receiver then turns over the proceeds to the wife as the court directs. The receiver's function is similar to that of a receiver in bankruptcy.

tenancy, joint: A joint tenancy is ownership of real or personal property (e.g., house, bank account, stocks) in the name of both parties with provision that if one dies, the other becomes sole owner. Banks and stock companies usually indicate joint tenancy by an expression that reads, "John Doe and/or Mary Doe as joint tenants with right of survivorship. . . ." If one joint tenant dies, the other becomes the sole owner. In a joint tenancy, either party has the power to transfer his share of the property without the knowledge of the other, even though it may not be right to do so. Such a transfer to a buyer without notice of the true state of affairs is an effective transfer of his interest in the property.

tenancy by the entirety: Property owned by a husband and wife together. The property is treated as though owned by one person, and, as in joint tenancy, the survivor takes all. Neither spouse can transfer the property legally without the consent of the other. If one spouse tries to transfer the whole property, the buyer gets only that spouse's share subject to forfeiture if the one who sold dies before the other spouse. A tenancy by the entirety can last no longer than the marriage. Death or divorce terminates it. Death transfers the whole ownership to the surviving spouse. Divorce converts the ownership into a tenancy in common.

tenancy in common: When two or more people own shares in property, they are tenants in common. When one dies, his or her share goes to his/her heirs. There is nothing to restrict a tenant in common from selling his/her share to a stranger; it is practically the same as owning shares in General Motors.

venue (compare with *geographical jurisdiction*): Venue is often confused with jurisdiction; but it is not the same. Venue relates to the place within the state or jurisdiction where the action should be tried. Often, in criminal trials, the defendant asks for a "change of venue" because he claims he cannot get a fair trial in a particular location (he is too well known; there has been unfair publicity). The court may change the venue by transferring the case to another court which has jurisdiction of the crime, but which is in a different part of the state.

Venue is based on political subdivisions of the state, such as counties. For matrimonial matters, the proper venue is generally the county in which one of the parties has his/her home, or where the cause of action arose. At that location, the supreme or superior court has jurisdiction to hear the case. In some states, the family court has been given similar jurisdiction.

Index